# CANAL HOUSE
# COOKING

CANAL HOUSE

No. 6 Coryell Street

Lambertville, NJ 08530

thecanalhouse.com


ISBN 978-0-9827-3944-0


Printed in China


Book design by CANAL HOUSE, a group of artists who collaborate on design projects.
This book was designed by Melissa Hamilton, Christopher Hirsheimer & Teresa Hopkins.
Edited by Margo True & Copyedited by Valerie Saint-Rossy.
Editorial assistance by Frani Beadle, Julia Lee, Julie Sproesser & Elizabeth May Wyckoff.


With great appreciation to
Colman Andrews, Lori di Mori & Jason Lowe


Distributed to the trade by
Andrews McMeel Publishing, LLC
an Andrews McMeel Universal Company
1130 Walnut Street, Kansas City, Missouri 64106

www.andrewsmcmeel.com

11 12 13 14 OGP 10 9 8 7 6 5 4 3 2 1


ATTENTION: SCHOOLS AND BUSINESSES

Andrews McMeel books are available at quantity discounts with bulk purchase for
educational, business, or sales promotional use. For information, please e-mail
the Andrews McMeel Publishing Special Sales Department:

specialsales@amuniversal.com

# CANAL HOUSE
# COOKING

Volume N° 7

Hamilton & Hirsheimer

Welcome to Canal House—our studio, workshop, dining room, office, kitchen, and atelier devoted to good ideas and good work relating to the world of food. We write, photograph, design, and paint, but in our hearts we both think of ourselves as cooks first.

Our loft studio is in an old red brick warehouse. A beautiful lazy canal runs alongside the building. We have a simple galley kitchen. Two small apartment-size stoves sit snugly side by side against a white tiled wall. We have a dishwasher, but prefer to hand wash the dishes so we can look out of the tall window next to the sink and see the ducks swimming in the canal or watch the raindrops splashing into the water.

And every day we cook. Starting in the morning we tell each other what we made for dinner the night before. Midday, we stop our work, set the table simply with paper napkins, and have lunch. We cook seasonally because that's what makes sense. So it came naturally to write down what we cook. The recipes in our books are what we make for ourselves and our families all year long. If you cook your way through a few, you'll see that who we are comes right through in the pages: that we are crazy for tomatoes in summer, make braises and stews all fall, and turn oranges into marmalade in winter.

*Canal House Cooking* is home cooking by home cooks for home cooks. We use ingredients found in most markets. All the recipes are easy to prepare for the novice and experienced cook alike. We want to share them with you as fellow cooks along with our love of food and all its rituals. The everyday practice of simple cooking and the enjoyment of eating are two of the greatest pleasures in life.

CHRISTOPHER HIRSHEIMER served as food and design editor for *Metropolitan Home* magazine, and was one of the founders of *Saveur* magazine, where she was executive editor. She is a writer and a photographer.

MELISSA HAMILTON cofounded the restaurant Hamilton's Grill Room in Lambertville, New Jersey, where she served as executive chef. She worked at *Martha Stewart Living, Cook's Illustrated,* and at *Saveur* as the food editor.

*Right: above, Melissa (left) and Christopher (right) in Siena; below, the Canal House ride*

## Tempus Fugit

the hinds head sacred gin & tonic 11, gin & limone 11, dazzling italian sparklers 12

## Working Up an Appetito

tramezzini: with white truffle butter 20, with prosciutto & arugula 21

speck, fontina & lemon panino 22, panino bianco 22

supplì al telefono 25, fonduta 26

bottarga on warm buttered toast 27, prosciutto & figs 27

## A Good Day for a Big Bowl of Zuppa

christmas soup 31, mussel soup 32

capon broth with anolini 33, minestrone 35

## Pasta

spinach pasta 38, egg pasta 38

green lasagne with tomato sauce & fresh ricotta 41, lasagne bolognese 41

fresh ricotta, butter & lemon ravioli 42, pappardelle & mushrooms 43

spinach tagliatelle with simple tomato sauce & ricotta 45

gnocchi verdi 46, ricotta gnocchi 49

## Riso

risotto bianco 52, risotto milanese 53

risotto alla certosina 54, tummala di risotto e spinaci 57

## Pesce

stewed eel 61, oil-poached swordfish 63, salt cod with tomatoes & green olives 64

branzino with shrimp & fennel 65, squid & potatoes 66

### Big Birds & Little Rabbit
roast capon with dressing 70

chestnuts, prunes & bread crumbs 70, sausage & apples 71

poached capon in rich brodo 74, cold capon salad 74

roast guinea hen with cipolline & chestnuts 75

braised rabbit with capers & pancetta 77

### Carne
cabbage & fennel with sausages & borlotti 80

braised lamb & green beans 82, meatballs with mint & parsley 83

osso buco 86, new year's cotechino with lentils 87

### Eat Your Verdure
porcini in umido 90, cabbage in agrodolce 90, stuffed onions piedmontese 91

peppers in agrodolce 92, chickpeas with stewed tomatoes 94

zucca 95, warm salad of radicchio & white beans 99

celery baked with tomatoes 99

### Why Buy It When You Can Make It?
salsa verde 102, fresh whole milk ricotta 102, simple tomato sauce 103

balsamella 106, ragù bolognese 107

spinach tagliatelle bolognese 107, pappardelle bolognese 107

### Dolci
apple cake 111, jam tart 112, cheesecake from rome's jewish quarter 114

vin santo-poached pears with gorgonzola dolce 117, chocolate chestnut torte 118

monte bianco 121, gelato di gianduia 122

WE RENTED A FARMHOUSE IN TUSCANY—a remote, rustic old stucco and stone house at the end of a gravel road, deep in the folds of vine-covered hills. It had a stone terrace with a long table for dinners outside, a grape arbor, and apple and fig trees loaded with fruit in the garden. There was no phone, TV, or Internet service, just a record player and shelves and shelves of books. It had a spare, simple kitchen with a classic waist-high fireplace with a grill. It was all we had hoped for. It was our Casa Canale for a month.

The decision had been made back in our New Jersey studio six months earlier on a cold rainy day in early spring. Over a lunch of cannelloni, we'd gotten into a long conversation about why Italian food tastes so damn delicious. We sat there for a couple of hours discussing it. We have both traveled extensively in Italy, eating in every region, and in one sense we really do know Italian food: We know that *seppie* (cuttlefish) is served with white polenta in the Veneto; that bread crumbs replace grated cheese in Sicily; and that in Genoa, only tiny, sweet Genovese basil is used to make pesto—leaves grown in warmer climes are deemed too aggressive in flavor. But the more you learn, the less you know. And we realized that for all the times we'd been to Italy, there was still so much we wanted to understand about Italian home cooking. By the end of lunch we had a plan. We'd go to Italy, find a house with a kitchen, and cook. We looked at each other and laughed, surprised that we could imagine doing such a thing. But that's just what we did.

We arrived on a warm autumn afternoon. There was a note from our landlady —under a bottle of Chianti on the stone table outside the kitchen door—listing area restaurants, market schedules, where to shop, and where to find our morning cappuccino. There was no food in the house, and by now the shops were closed, so, following her advice, we put on our coats and walked down the road to buy vegetables from a nearby gardener. Evening was falling as we knocked on the door of a small house surrounded by a big garden. A man answered, and we could see he'd been enjoying an early dinner. We apologized for disturbing him but when we said we'd come to buy vegetables, he replied, "*Ma certo!*", and gestured toward the garden. Out we headed in the moonlight, into rows of silvery cardoons, as he motioned us to follow. We pointed at a big head of cabbage. He took his sharp sickle knife and thwacked it from its stalk. Then he harvested four heads of radicchio and some of the cardoons for us. We shook hands in the dark garden and then

*Previous pages: our home away from home, Casa Canale in Tuscany*

hurried up the road back to the safety of our farmhouse. We were thrilled at our good fortune; we never would have had this experience at home.

Early the next day, we hiked over the hill and through the woods to find the caffè-bar and a market. As we came into the village, we passed a garage with the door rolled up and noticed two aproned women standing on either side of a table, chatting away as they plucked a pile of chickens. We walked over to get a closer look and noticed a particularly big bird. "*Cappone,*" said the older lady, confirming our hopes that it was a capon. Money was exchanged and the bird went right into our market bag. We bought chestnuts at the market, and our first proper Italian meal was roasted capon with chestnut stuffing, spit-roasted in the fireplace.

Every day we had small adventures. Driving through the countryside, we'd stop at markets, dairies, and wineries to check everything out. Along the way, we'd gather what looked good to cook for our dinner. We preferred to eat out for lunch; it was more fun, and then we didn't have to brave the narrow, winding roads after dark. We'd peek inside the kitchens of the restaurants where we ate. More often than not, it was women in white cooks' smocks who were manning the stoves, tending big pots of *ragù* and cutting and filling *anolini* from smooth sheets of fresh pasta.

The big, rich flavors of fall were coming through the markets and farms and into our kitchen. We cooked with chestnuts, rabbit, porcini, pumpkin, cabbage, peppers, radicchio, apples, and pears. Like the Italians, we developed flavors as we cooked. We fried *battuto*—onions, carrots, and celery—into fragrant *soffrito*; toasted tomato paste to add color and richness to sauces; deglazed pans with red wine, allowing it to reduce to its very essence; and we balanced sweet and sour in *agrodolce*.

We know that cooking is not only about ingredients and techniques. Recipes have a spirit, they are born of a place and a culture, and to cook well you have to be sensitive to and honor that spirit. Italians are refined traditionalists; they want their *ragù bolognese* served with *parmiagano-reggiano* and never *pecorino romano*. It just wouldn't taste right otherwise. They are generous, too: It's evident in the way they cook. They pour olive oil liberally, shave white truffles with abandon, toss their pasta in the sauce, dress salads by feel—and they have a word for it: *abbondanza*.

Then one day we found ourselves in Florence in a beautiful wine bar, Procacci, drinking prosecco and eating *panini tartufati*—but we were melancholy. We were ready to go home to the real Canal House and start cooking Italian food our way. And that's just what we did.

Christopher & Melissa

*Previous pages: left, Amalfi Coast lemons; right, Cibrèo Caffè, Florence. This page: a prized corner table at Harry's Bar in Venice*

## THE HINDS HEAD SACRED GIN & TONIC

On our way to Italy we were bumped off a connecting flight from London to Venice and found ourselves stuck in an airport hotel for the night. Instead of an icy martini and carpaccio at Harry's Bar, it appeared we would be pushing Grilled Chicken Caesar around our dinner plates. We put out a call to our London friend Jason Lowe, and he knew just what we should do, "Take a taxi to Bray, it is only ten miles from Heathrow, and have dinner at Heston Blumenthal's other place, The Hinds Head." Too late for reservations, would we ever get in? The dice were thrown, a taxi was called, and when we walked in the door of the charming 400-year-old village pub, we spotted an empty table for two. We sat our lucky seats right in the seats and were soon sipping authentic London hand-distilled Sacred Gin, so delicate it reminded us of *sake*. They brought us little bottles of crisp, sharp tonic water and fat lemon wedges, which we eventually mixed with the gin. Raw, purebred Hereford beef with radicchio and horseradish was on the menu for dinner. Happenstance is often far better than *any* plan. ——CH

## GIN & LIMONE

One evening, a week into our stay at our idyllic but rather remote Tuscan farmhouse, an *apertivo* sounded mighty good. But since there wasn't a drop in the house, we headed off in search of some charming little bar, somewhere in a charming little town nearby. We drove into Impruneta and spotted a bustling caffè, but it was *festivale* season—the town was packed and parking impossible. We ended up, of all places, at a Coop supermarket, where there was lots of parking available. We found a bottle of Beefeater gin, but there was neither a bottle of tonic nor a single lime, and when we asked for ice, they showed us ice cream. We bought the gin, but what to do about the ice? I told Christopher that since I didn't remember seeing any ice cubes in the bare freezer, I could simply pour the gin over the ice-cold wire coils in the freezer to chill it—although that did sound a bit desperate. But Fortuna smiled on us. In the back of the bottom drawer of the freezer was a tiny six-cube tray with ice. Three cubes went into each glass, then the gin (2 ounces in each), and in place of tonic, I squeezed in the juice of an Amalfi Coast lemon as big as a baseball and garnished each drink with a twist. Sometimes, things that taste good when you're away don't measure up when you return home. This cocktail hits the spot in either place. ——MH

DAZZLING ITALIAN SPARKLERS

BY

COLMAN ANDREWS

ACK WHEN I BEGAN DISCOVERING WINE, shortly after Noah planted that first postdiluvian grapevine, it was considered vaguely racy and vaguely suave to order something called Asti Spumante. This was a frothy Italian sparkler whose principal virtues seemed to be low price and high sugar. It was undeniably a step up from the "crackling rosé" then being foisted on the drinking public by Paul Masson and other firms, but it always sort of made my teeth ache.

A little later, America (except at my house) came under the spell of another carbonated *italiano*, Lambrusco—specifically the soda-popish versions turned out by the Cantine Cooperative Riunite in the Emilia region, which became our nation's number-one vinous import, no doubt thanks, at least partially, to having been promoted under one of the more annoyingly unforgettable advertising slogans of the late 1970s and early 1980s: "Riunite on ice. That's nice."

At least partially because of my brief experiences with these two varieties of vino, I pretty much crossed Italian sparklers off my personal wine list. I'd enjoy a Soave or Chianti or Gattinara now and then, but if I wanted something with bubbles, I'd stick to France or maybe California in a pinch (and later still, to Spain, after that country's cavas started flooding into the country, pretty much washing away any other sparkler in the lower price range).

Then I started logging serious time in Italy, and my perceptions began to change. I discovered that *spumante* was simply the Italian word for bubbly, and that Asti was a commune in Piedmont, capable of producing not just the less than pleasant plonk of my earlier experience but also examples (exclusively from the Moscato Bianco grape)

of great charm, low in alcohol, delightfully fruity, and while undeniably sweet, not necessarily cloying. (Asti Spumante's cousin, Moscato d'Asti, has lighter carbonation —it is called *frizzante*, fizzy, rather than spumante—and even less alcohol.)

And that turned out to be just the beginning. I also encountered very nice Chardonnay-based sparkling wine, made by the *"metodo champenoise"* (Champagne method) in Trento, in the region called Trentino-Alto Adige. (That term is no longer legal, incidentally; such wines are now *"metodo classico"*.) I became a big fan of the crisp, coolly elegant (if ambitiously priced) sparkling wines made by the effervescent Maurizio Zanella of Ca' del Bosco in Erbusco, in the Franciacorta region of Lombardy—not least because I got to know him, visited his winery several times, and even got invited to his wedding. (I brought home a magnum of his special Prestige Cuvée that I drank at my own wedding rehearsal dinner; it was certainly one of the best non-Champagne sparkling wines I've ever had.) Bellavista is another notable producer in the area, while Levi Dalton, wine director at Bar Boulud in Manhattan and a serious Italian wine lover, prefers smaller producers like Barone Pizzini and Wertmuller.

Elsewhere, I joined Venetian friends in their home city to quaff Prosecco— made (like the sparklers of Asti) by the Charmat tank-fermenting method in the Veneto and Friuli-Venezia Giulia (and especially the bailiwicks of Conegliano and Valdobbiadene)—and found various interpretations of the wine to be, well, not exactly profound but certainly frivolously attractive and all too easy to drink. (Mionetto is the most widely sold brand in the United States, but not necessarily my favorite. Try Sommariva or maybe Sacchetto.)

I soon came to realize, in fact, that wines with varying degrees of sparkle, made by several different techniques, out of many different grapes, and in a whole bouquet of styles, are produced all over Italy. A non–Asti Spumante from Emilia, highly recommended by Levi Dalton, is Alberto Tedeschi's Pignoletto Spungola Bellaria (the grape is the little-known Pignoletto). Dalton likes the metodo classico wines, also from Emilia, from Francesco Bellei e C. and the Paolo Rinaldini "Orom" Bianco Brut NV. "One imagines that few make wines like this anymore, from anywhere in the world"—and calls the Camillo Donati Malvasia Secco Frizzante "one of my favorite wines from Italy." Bruce Neyers, national sales director for Kermit Lynch, the Berkeley wine importer of cult status, is proud to sell Elvio Tinero's frizzante wines, one made from Moscato,

*Overleaf: Volpaia, Tuscany*

one from the local Favorita variety. He also adds to the repertoire a couple of wines, a spumante and a frizzante, from Punta Crena in Liguria.

In Piedmont, Bartolo Mascarello turns the Freisa grape into an ebullient frizzante. The estimable Darrell Corti of Corti Bros. in Sacramento notes that at one time, there was even bubbly Chianti. "Chianti was sold 'fresco di governo'," he explains, "which meant that it had some $CO_2$ and was lively on the tongue. This style is now forgotten about and should be reexamined. It is sort of a nouveau wine with more character."

And then there's…Lambrusco. The first time I went to Parma, to do a story on the local cheese (of which you have heard), I was invited to lunch by a prominent local Parmigiano producer. He took me to his favorite trattoria, where he began by ordering plates of prosciutto and Parma salame, then fairly shocked me by asking for a bottle of Lambrusco to go with them. It was as if, I thought, some French Brie producer had taken me to a neighborhood bistro and ordered Coke. What was the guy thinking? He must have sensed my perplexity, and said, "This is not the Lambrusco you know in America. This is real wine, and we believe that you need something like this in order to help digest all the pork fat we eat here."

I took a sip of what the waiter brought and immediately realized that "something like this" meant a wine that could be deep gorgeous garnet-black in color, rich and creamy, jauntily acidic, and redolent of juicy grapes and black plums, with an almost dry finish (though the wine can sometimes be a little sweet); oh, and not exactly bubbles but a pinpoint fizz that seemed to make its flavor dance. In other words, rather unusual and really good. But don't take my word for it. There's plenty of high-quality Lambrusco around today in America. Bruce Neyer's company imports Moretto's bone-dry, full-flavored Lambrusco Secco. Levi Dalton likes the stylish Vigneto Saetti "Vigna Ca' del Fiore" and loves Graziano's "Fontana dei Boschi" Modena Lambrusco di Castelvetro, which he calls "Awesome!" and "a total original". Me, I'm partial to Cantine Ceci "La Luna", just bursting with fruit, and to Grasparossa di Castelvetro from Cleto Chiarli, one of the oldest Lambrusco producers—a wine that's lean and dark, intensely grapey, and just delicious. It doesn't sparkle, it dazzles.

Colman Andrews, our dear friend and mentor, was a cofounder of *Saveur* and is now editorial director of *thedailymeal.com*.

working up an appetito

## TRAMEZZINI & PANINI

There always seems to be a good sandwich to be had in Italy no matter where you are. You find them—the crustless-white-bread *tramezzini* and all variety of *panini* (stuffed rolls or buns, pressed on a griddle or not)—at every caffè-bar, at airports big and small, even at filling stations along the *autostrada*. Whenever we're in Florence, we head to Cebrèo Caffè near the Mercato di Sant'Ambrogio for a morning cappuccino and one of their delicious little panini with sweet butter and prosciutto, and at the end of the day to the demurely elegant food shop and wine bar Procacci for a glass of something sparkling and a couple of their famous *panini tartufati*. Our recipes for these little sandwiches are inspired by these two favorites.

We've not been able to find tender sweet rolls like we ate in Italy, so we use slices of challah or brioche, or thin slices of white sandwich bread for these sandwiches. They'll keep, well covered, in a cool spot (they'll taste better if you don't refrigerate them) for up to 4 hours.

## WHITE TRUFFLE BUTTER TRAMEZZINI

As odd as it may seem, we prefer the quality of Kerrygold Irish butter to the imported butters from Italy for these sandwiches. If you happen to have a white truffle, shave some of it into softened butter to make this spread. Chances are you don't, so use white truffle paste instead. It comes in a convenient tube—a little goes a long way. The Italian truffle company Urbani is a good source. You can also buy truffle butter, but the flavor won't be as fresh as making your own.

Beat 8 tablespoons room temperature unsalted butter in a bowl with an electric mixer on medium-high speed until light and fluffy, 1–2 minutes. Stir in 2 teaspoons white truffle paste and season it with a little sea salt. Set the butter aside. We use 1–2 tablespoons butter per sandwich. Use more or less to suit your taste. ——*makes 8–12 half-sandwiches*

VERY THIN WHITE BREAD TRAMEZZINI: Trim the crust off 3 slices very thin white sandwich bread. Spread some of the white truffle butter on 2 of the slices of bread. To make this double-decker sandwich, place one of the slices of buttered bread on top of the other, buttered side up, and finish the sandwich with the third slice of bread. Cut the sandwich in half on the diagonal. ——*makes 2 half-sandwiches*

CHALLAH OR BRIOCHE TRAMEZZINI: Use 2 thin slices challah or brioche. Spread some of the white truffle butter on one slice, top with the other slice, and cut the sandwich in half. ——*makes 2 half-sandwiches*

## PROSCIUTTO & ARUGULA TRAMEZZINI

When we make these *tramezzini* with plainer white sandwich bread, we like to add peppery arugula leaves. But when making them with challah or brioche, we like to keep the flavors pure—just the whipped sweet butter, the nutty cured ham, and the tender bread.

Beat 8 tablespoons room temperature unsalted butter in a bowl with an electric mixer on medium-high speed until light and fluffy, 1–2 minutes. Set the butter aside. We use 1–2 tablespoons butter per sandwich. Use more or less to suit your taste. ——*makes 8–12 half-sandwiches*

VERY THIN WHITE BREAD TRAMEZZINI: Trim the crust off 3 slices very thin white sandwich bread. Spread some of the whipped butter on the bread. To make this double-decker sandwich, drape 1 thin slice Prosciutto di Parma on each of 2 slices of the buttered bread and top them with small arugula leaves. Stack on top of each other, arugula side up, and top with the third slice of bread, buttered side down. Cut the sandwich in half on the diagonal with a very sharp knife. ——*makes 2 half-sandwiches*

CHALLAH OR BRIOCHE TRAMEZZINI: Spread 2 thin slices challah or brioche with some of the whipped butter. Drape 2 thin slices Prosciutto di Parma over one of the slices of bread and top the sandwich with the other slice, buttered side down. Cut the sandwich in half with a very sharp knife. ——*makes 2 half-sandwiches*

## SPECK, FONTINA & LEMON PANINO

We like a thin, spare grilled panino with a glass of wine at the end of the day. We've seen many recipes that use slices of crusty ciabatta, but we prefer the softer crust and more delicate crumb of focaccia to make ours.

Take a 4-inch square of focaccia and cut off each crust horizontally so that the 2 slices have ½ inch of white still attached. Brush the crust side of each piece with extra-virgin olive oil. Put 4 thin slices speck or Prosciutto di Parma, then several thin slices Fontina Valle d'Aosta on the cut side of the bottom piece of focaccia. Add a light grating of fresh lemon zest and some cracked black pepper. Top the sandwich with the other piece of focaccia, crust side up.

Cook the sandwich in an electric or stovetop panini press until the cheese melts and the crust is crisp and golden brown, about 5 minutes. Or, if you don't have a panini press, place the sandwich on a warm, lightly oiled griddle or cast-iron skillet over medium heat. Set another heavy pan on top of the sandwich to weigh it down. Cook the sandwich until golden brown on the bottom, 3–5 minutes. Turn the sandwich over, weighing it down with the second pan, and cook the panino until the cheese melts and the second side is golden, about 2 minutes. Cut the panino in half on the diagonal and serve straightaway. —— *serves 1*

## PANINO BIANCO

Follow the directions above for preparing two thin-crusted pieces of focaccia for the panino. Spread the bottom piece of focaccia with 2 tablespoons mascarpone. Lay 2–3 thin slices Robiola on top. Spread ½ teaspoon white truffle paste over the cheese, then grate Grana Padano on top. Top the sandwich with the second piece of focaccia, crust side up, and continue with the directions above for cooking the panino. —— *serves 1*

# SUPPLÌ AL TELEFONO
makes 12–16

*Supplì*, fried rice croquettes, are a Roman specialty. The whimsical *telefono* refers to the strings of melted cheese, resembling telephone wires, that ooze from the center of a croquette as you bite into it. We keep our supplì making simple, using leftover risotto, but we also use cold cooked rice mixed with ragù, parmigiano, and herbs. These small crisp bites are perfect with an *aperitivo*.

Sicilian *arancini*, "little oranges", are hearty rice croquettes. They are usually filled with *balsamella* and peas, ragù, or a mixture of both. We found these popular snacks in corner bars and home kitchens across Sicily. Use this supplì recipe to make larger croquettes and fill them with whatever you like. They are always best when served right after they're fried.

| | |
|---|---|
| 3 cups cold risotto, milanese or bianco (pages 52–53) | 1 cup flour |
| 3 eggs | 1–2 cups panko or fine dried bread crumbs |
| ¾ cup parmigiano-reggiano | Vegetable oil |
| 12–16 cubes mozzarella, ½-inch | Salt |

Mix together the risotto, 1 of the eggs, and the parmigiano in a bowl. Wet your hands with cold water so the rice will not stick to them as you work. Put 1 generous tablespoon risotto in the middle of your palm. Press a cube of mozzarella into the rice. Work the rice around the cheese to cover it completely to keep it from oozing out as you fry it. Add a little extra rice if needed. Press the rice balls into oval shapes. Arrange the balls in a single layer on a tray. Put the flour, remaining 2 eggs, and the panko in separate shallow bowls. Beat the eggs with a few tablespoons water. Roll each ball first in flour, then in egg, and finally in panko. Arrange the coated supplì in a single layer on the same tray. At this point you can cover them with plastic, and refrigerate until you are ready to fry them.

Add enough oil to a heavy large skillet to reach a depth of 2 inches. Heat over medium-high heat to a temperature of 350°. Or, if a wooden chopstick dipped into the bottom of the oil sends bubbles up right away, the oil is ready for frying. Fry the supplì in the oil, turning them as they cook, until golden on all sides. Drain on a wire rack. Season with salt.

# FONDUTA
## serves 6–8

I remember going to Italy years ago specifically to eat white truffles—my first food pilgrimage. It was October and as we drove through the rolling Piedmontese countryside, the scenery was storybook. Farmers were harvesting their grapes from hillside vineyards, the leaves on the trees were golden, and so was the afternoon light—it was all drowsy and dreamy. But the pretty town of Alba was bustling, its annual White Truffle Festival was in full swing. The streets were filled with strolling food lovers from all over the world, seeking a whiff and a taste of the famed *Tuber magnatum*. We headed for the truffle dealers' tent in the Mercado del Tartufo. In the midst of the selling floor, with all its great-looking characters on both sides of the counters, was a booth serving fonduta. Authentic Piedmontese fonduta is the ultimate of melted cheese dishes, made with rich, semisoft straw-colored Fontina Valle d'Aosta—earthy, herbaceous, and nutty. I ordered and the server spooned warm fonduta into a gratin dish, slid on an orange-yolked egg fried in butter, then shaved a shower of white truffles on top until I said, "*Basta!*" Today we serve little dishes of fonduta, truffle or no truffle, with crisp crostini and glasses of cold Arneis. ——CH

4 tablespoons butter
4 egg yolks, well beaten
1 cup whole milk
1 pound Fontina Valle d'Aosta, grated

Ground white pepper
A white truffle as large as your
     pocketbook will bear, optional
Piles of crostini

Melt the butter in the top of a double boiler (or in a saucepan set in a larger pot) set over, not in, barely simmering water over low heat. Whisk the yolks and the milk together in a bowl. Stir in the cheese. Gradually add the milk and cheese to the melted butter, gently whisking (it may separate and thin; keep whisking), until everything has melted into a smooth, thick cream, 10–15 minutes.

Spoon into warmed soup plates, season generously with white pepper, shower with thinly sliced white truffle (if you are lucky enough to have one), and serve with lots of crostini.

VARIATION: Put wedges of fried polenta onto each plate and spoon warm fonduta over the polenta. Shave on thin slices of white truffle, if you like.

## BOTTARGA ON WARM BUTTERED TOAST

We keep a package of bottarga, the dried roe of tuna or gray mullet that is a specialty of Sicilian and Sardinian cooking, in our refrigerator at the ready to shave over pasta or to make these quick little antipasti if friends drop by at the end of the day.

Toast thin slices of crusty country white bread and spread the warm toast with good unsalted butter. Lay several very thin slices bottarga on top of each. Serve while the toast is warm, with a small wedge or two of lemon for squeezing a bit of juice on the bottarga. ——*makes as many as you like*

## PROSCIUTTO & FIGS

Our dear friend David Tanis—wonderful writer, chef, and one of the best cooks in the world—wrote *A Platter of Figs and Other Recipes* (Artisan, 2008). That was a pretty funny and ironic title since it was a cookbook and a platter of figs needs no recipe it's so simple. But of course, think of all the knowledge and experience you need to choose the perfect fig. That's what makes a really good cook, a deep knowledge and understanding of ingredients, and a real feel for their nature.

Here's what we know: Fall figs are smaller and sweeter than those you'll find in the early summer. Figs are best if they are allowed to ripen on the tree before being picked, so buy them at farmers' markets. Perfectly ripe, they will have a small drop of fig nectar at the blossom end, which the Italians call, "the tear in the eye". These beautiful fruit come in a range of skin colors, from purplish-black to bronze to bright green, with pink to purple flesh. In this classic antipasto, Italians pair the sweet luscious fig flavor against the salty pork of thinly sliced prosciutto di Parma.

We allow 2 ripe figs (cut into quarters attached at the stem end) and 2 slices of prosciutto di Parma per person. Arrange everything on a large platter and serve, either with napkins (if people will be eating out of hand) or, with small plates, and knives and forks. ——*serves as many as you like*

a good day for a big bowl of zuppa

# CHRISTMAS SOUP
## serves 8

This lovely soup is a traditional holiday *primo*. Escarole is one of the cold weather lettuces with the good bitter flavor that Italians love. We toss it in salads, sauté it in olive oil, and simmer it in broth—as we do in this soup.

1 chicken, 3 pounds, cut into 8 pieces
2 onions, peeled and quartered
Peel of 1 lemon
2 bay leaves
Salt

10 black peppercorns
1 bottle white wine
Freshly ground black pepper
2 heads escarole, trimmed and sliced into 1-inch strips
Parmigiano-reggiano

Arrange the chicken legs, thighs, wings, and back in a heavy large pot over medium heat. Cover and cook, stirring occasionally, until some of the fat and juices have been released, 15–20 minutes. Add the onions, keeping them intact, lemon peel, bay leaves, 2 teaspoons salt, and the peppercorns. Place the breasts on top. Add the wine, then enough water to cover everything by 3 inches. Bring to a boil over medium-high heat. Reduce the heat to low, and barely simmer the broth. Skim off any foam that rises to the surface. Cover with the lid slightly ajar.

After the broth has simmered for 20 minutes, remove the chicken breasts and set aside on a plate to cool. Continue cooking the broth for 40 minutes. Remove the onions, taking care to kept them intact, and set aside on a plate. Remove the chicken parts from the pot and set aside on a plate to cool. When cool enough to handle, pull the meat from the bones. Discard the bones.

While the chicken cools, strain the broth through a fine-mesh sieve into a bowl. Wash out the pot and pour the broth back in. Taste and season with salt and pepper. Add the escarole and cook over medium heat until it wilts, 5 minutes. Serve the chicken, onions, escarole, and broth in warm wide soup bowls with lots of grated parmigiano.

*Overleaf: Ponte Vecchio in Florence*

# MUSSEL SOUP
### serves 6

This flavorful mussel soup, Italian in spirit but with New World influences, has the tomatoey richness of a good Manhattan clam chowder.

1 onion, chopped

3 cloves garlic, chopped

1 teaspoon fennel seeds

½ teaspoon crushed red pepper flakes

1 bottle white wine

2 pounds mussels, debearded

6 tablespoons extra-virgin olive oil

1 fennel bulb with fronds, bulb finely diced and fronds chopped

1 russet potato, peeled and diced

4 cups Simple Tomato Sauce (page 103) or passata di pomodoro

Salt and pepper

Put the onions, garlic, fennel seeds, pepper flakes, and wine into a large pot, cover, and simmer over medium-high heat for 10 minutes. Add the mussels, cover the pot, and steam them, shaking the pot from time to time, until the shells have opened, 5–10 minutes.

Strain the broth through a fine-mesh sieve into a large bowl, catching the mussels. Pick the mussels from the shells, put them into another bowl, and discard the shells and any unopened mussels. Cover the mussels and refrigerate.

Heat the olive oil in a heavy medium pot over medium heat. Add the diced fennel, cover, and cook until soft, 5–10 minutes. Add the potatoes and tomato sauce, then add the reserved mussel broth (leave behind any grit in the bottom of the bowl). Cover and simmer until the potatoes are tender, about 20 minutes.

Reduce the heat to medium-low. Add the mussels and chopped fennel fronds and simmer until the mussels are heated through. Season to taste with salt and pepper. Ladle the soup into bowls and drizzle with a little olive oil, if you like. Serve with hot crusty bread.

# CAPON BROTH WITH ANOLINI
## serves 8

This small stuffed pasta, typical of Parma, is shaped with an anolini cutter into fluted rounds, or into half-moons, and cooked in broth even when served sauced. We prepare this dish during the holidays—the little pasta packages are the kind of gifts we're interested in giving these days. Tortellini, another Bolognese pasta served in broth, can be substituted for anolini.

FOR THE ANOLINI
1 tablespoon extra-virgin olive oil
½ small onion, minced
1 small clove garlic, minced
4 ounces ground chicken
4 ounces ground pork
4 ounces ground veal
1 cup grated parmigiano-reggiano, plus more for serving

2–3 pinches of nutmeg
Salt and pepper
1 egg, lightly beaten
½ pound Egg Pasta (page 38)
Flour

12–14 cups capon broth from Poached Capon in Rich Brodo (page 74) or rich poultry broth

For the anolini, heat the oil in a medium skillet over medium heat. Add the onions and garlic, and cook until soft, 3–5 minutes. Add the meats and cook, breaking it up with a spoon, until the liquid evaporates, 5–10 minutes. Pulse the mixture in a food processor briefly until it begins to hold together, but doesn't become a paste. Transfer to a mixing bowl. Add the parmigiano and nutmeg, and season well with salt and pepper. Add the egg and mix well. Set filling aside.

Roll 1 piece of egg pasta dough out and lay it on a lightly floured surface. Use an inverted glass or a biscuit cutter to cut out 2-inch rounds. Put 1 scant teaspoon of filling on each round, fold it in half, and press the edge to seal in the filling. Put the anolini on lightly floured kitchen towels on trays in a single layer; cover with more towels. Repeat until the dough and filling are finished, making 80–100 anolini.

Put the broth into a large pot, season with salt, and bring to a boil. Add the anolini and simmer over medium heat, stirring occasionally, until tender, 4–5 minutes. Serve in wide soup bowls, grating parmigiano over each serving.

# MINESTRONE
## serves 6

Like most versions of this familiar soup, we follow and change ours with the seasons. It plays off what's available from our gardens or at the market. But generally speaking, we make our soup with fewer vegetables than more, and like it a little brothier rather than dense and stewy. We use small pasta like ditalini (little thimbles) that are no bigger than the cut of the vegetables. Minestrone alla Genovese includes the famous sauce from that region, pesto, and we often add a spoonful of that, or a version thereof, to ours.

¼ cup extra-virgin olive oil
1 medium onion, chopped
2 cloves garlic, finely chopped
2 tablespoons tomato paste
8 cups chicken stock
1 pound fresh Romano beans, cut into 1-inch pieces

1 pound baby zucchini, sliced into thick rounds
Salt and pepper
1 cup ditalini
1 cup Salsa Verde (page 102) or pesto

Heat the olive oil in a large pot over medium heat. Add the onions and cook, stirring often, until soft and translucent, about 5 minutes. Add the garlic, then stir in the tomato paste and cook for about 1 minute.

Add the chicken stock, Romano beans, and zucchini. Simmer the soup until the vegetables are tender, about 45 minutes. Season with salt and pepper.

Bring a medium pot of salted water to a boil over high heat. Add the pasta and cook, stirring occasionally, until just cooked through, 8–10 minutes. Drain the pasta, add it to the soup, and simmer for about 15 minutes longer.

Serve the soup, adding a spoonful or two of salsa verde to each bowl.

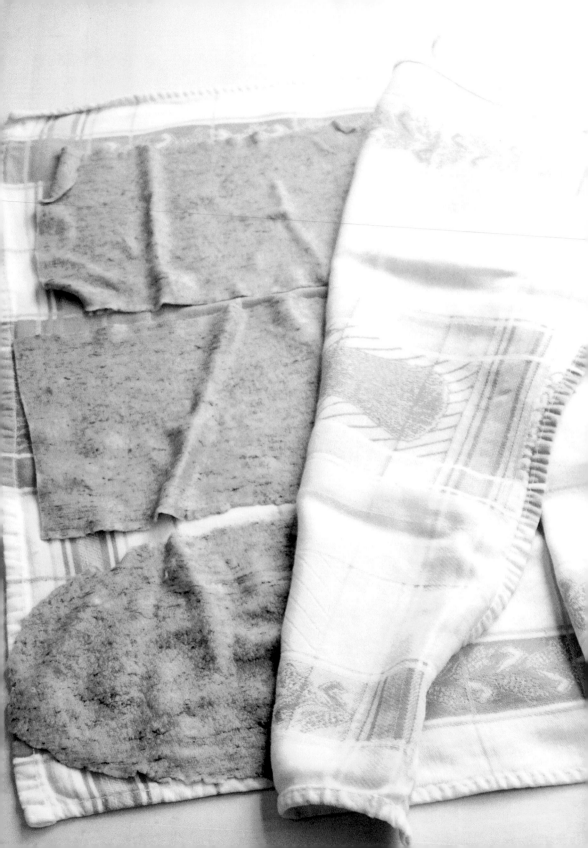

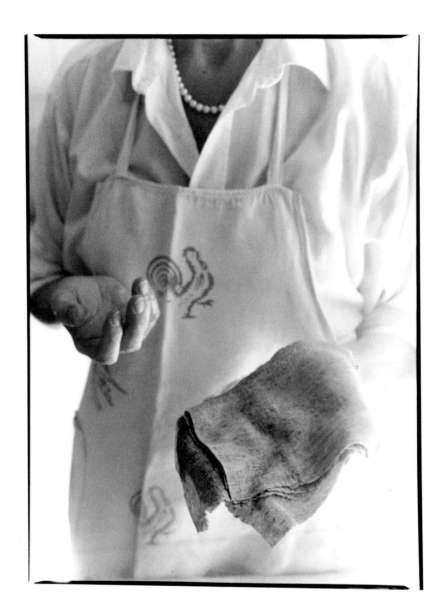

pasta

# SPINACH PASTA
## makes 1 pound

Italian wheat flour is graded by degrees of refining; "00" is the finest and used to make homemade pasta. Unbleached, all-purpose flour is a perfectly good substitute. Use mature spinach as "baby" leaves are too watery and tender.

1 pound spinach, washed and trimmed

Salt

2 cups "00" or unbleached all-purpose flour, plus more for dusting

2 extra-large eggs

Blanch the spinach in a large pot of salted boiling water for 1 minute. Transfer it with a slotted spoon to a bowl of ice water to cool, then drain it. Squeeze out as much water as possible with your hands. Finely chop the spinach.

Sift the flour into a mound on a smooth surface and make a well in the center. Add the spinach, then the eggs, and 1 generous pinch of salt to the well and beat with a fork until well combined. Continue gently beating the eggs and spinach while gradually stirring in the flour, little by little, from the inside rim of the well. When the dough is too lumpy to work with the fork, use your hands to knead in the remaining flour and form a rough ball.

Clean the work surface and lightly dust with flour. With clean hands, knead the dough, dusting it with flour as you work, into a smooth ball that is slightly tacky in the center, 3–4 minutes. Press your thumb into the center of the dough; if dough feels sticky, knead in a little more flour. Cover dough and let it rest at room temperature for 30 minutes or up to 3 hours.

Cut the dough into eighths and keep them covered. Flatten one piece of dough into a rectangle then feed it through the smooth cylinders of a hand-crank pasta machine set on the widest setting. Do this 2–3 times. Decrease the setting on the machine by one notch and feed the dough through the cylinders again. Repeat, decreasing the setting by one notch each time. Roll the pasta through all but the last notch. Lay the sheets of pasta out on a lightly floured surface and cover with clean, damp, kitchen towels.

EGG PASTA: Follow the directions above for making Spinach Pasta, omitting the spinach and using 3 extra-large eggs.

*Above: top, Green Lasagne with Tomato Sauce & Fresh Ricotta; bottom, Lasagne Bolognese*

# GREEN LASAGNE WITH TOMATO SAUCE & FRESH RICOTTA
## serves 8–12

The Simili twins of Bologna, Margherita and Valeria, legendary home cooks, taught us the nuances of making pasta and lasagne. It's their recipes we model ours on. Don't be hesitant to make sheets of fresh pasta for this noble layered dish; you need only take one bite of it to understand the difference between ordinary and sublime. If you've only had those clunky lasagne made with thick sheets of dried pasta, the tenderness of fresh pasta will be a revelation.

1 pound Spinach Pasta (page 38)
Salt
2 tablespoons butter
3 cups Simple Tomato Sauce (page 103)

1¼ cups grated parmigiano-reggiano
4 cups warm Balsamella (page 106)
1 cup fresh whole milk ricotta (page 102)

Cook the pasta, 1–2 sheets at a time, in a large pot of salted boiling water until tender, about 30 seconds. Carefully transfer the pasta to a bowl of ice water to cool. Lay the sheets of cooked pasta out on clean, damp, kitchen towels in a single layer without touching. Cover with more damp kitchen towels.

Preheat the oven to 400°. Grease a deep 9 × 13-inch baking dish with butter. Cover the bottom with a layer of pasta, trimming the sheets to fit and patching, if necessary. Spread evenly with 1 cup of the tomato sauce, then sprinkle with ¼ cup of the parmigiano. Add another layer of pasta, cover with 1½ cups of the balsamella, dot with ½ cup of the ricotta, then sprinkle with more parmigiano. Repeat layers again. Finally, add another layer of pasta, cover it with the remaining tomato sauce, then spoonfuls of the balsamella, and the parmigiano.

Bake lasagne until it is bubbling around the edges and browned on top, about 15 minutes. Do not overcook. Let lasagne rest for 10–15 minutes before serving.

# LASAGNE BOLOGNESE
## serves 8–12

Traditional *lasagne bolognese* is made with spinach pasta but we use either spinach or egg pasta depending on what we have. It's the ragù that matters.

*continued*

1 pound Spinach or Egg Pasta
  (page 38)
Salt
2 tablespoons butter

4–5 cups warm Ragù Bolognese
  (page 107)
1¼ cups grated parmigiano-reggiano
4 cups warm Balsamella (page 106)

Cook the pasta, 1–2 sheets at a time, in a large pot of salted boiling water until tender, about 30 seconds. Carefully transfer the pasta to a bowl of ice water to cool. Lay the sheets of cooked pasta out on clean, damp, kitchen towels in a single layer without touching. Cover with more damp kitchen towels.

Preheat the oven to 400°. Grease a deep 9 × 13-inch baking dish with butter. Cover the bottom with a layer of pasta, trimming the sheets to fit and patching, if necessary. Spread evenly with 1½ cups of the ragù, then sprinkle with ¼ cup of the parmigiano. Add another layer of pasta, cover it with 1½ cups of the balsamella, then sprinkle with more parmigiano. Repeat layers again. Add the final layer of pasta, cover it with the remaining ragù, then with the remaining balsamella, and sprinkle the last bit of parmigiano on top.

Bake lasagne until it is bubbling around the edges and browned on top, about 15 minutes. Do not overcook. Let lasagne rest for 10–15 minutes before serving.

## FRESH RICOTTA, BUTTER & LEMON RAVIOLI
### makes about 32

Freeze any uncooked ravioli on a lightly floured tray in a single layer, then store them in a covered container. When you're ready to cook the ravioli, just slip them straight from the freezer into salted boiling water.

FOR THE RAVIOLI
8 tablespoons softened butter
1 cup fresh whole milk ricotta
  (page 102)
½ cup grated parmigiano-reggiano
Grated zest of 1 lemon
Salt and pepper

1 pound Spinach or Egg Pasta
  (page 38)
Flour

FOR THE SAUCE
Butter
Parmigiano-reggiano

For the ravioli, put the butter, ricotta, parmigiano, and lemon zest into a bowl and mix well. Season the filling with salt and pepper to taste. Set aside.

Lay 1 sheet of pasta out on a lightly floured surface, keeping the other sheets in a single layer without touching, covered with damp kitchen towels. Put about 1 tablespoon of the filling about 2 inches apart in rows along the sheet of pasta. Using a pastry brush dipped in water, paint a grid around the mounds of filling. Lay another sheet of pasta on top and press down around the mounds to force out any air and to seal in the filling. Use an inverted glass or biscuit cutter to cut out 3-inch-round ravioli, or a fluted pastry wheel or sharp knife to cut ravioli into squares. Seal edges with the tines of a fork. Repeat with remaining pasta and filling. Cook 6–8 ravioli at a time in a large pot of salted boiling water until tender, 4–5 minutes. Transfer them with a slotted spoon to warm plates or a platter.

For the sauce, while the ravioli are still piping hot, put some big knobs of butter on them, add a spoonful or two of the hot pasta cooking water to melt the butter and moisten the pasta, then grate lots of parmigiano on top.

---

CUTTING PASTA ❧ Just rolled-out sheets of pasta are satiny smooth and soft—perfect for a good seal when making stuffed pastas like ravioli. To cut long strands for pappardelle or tagliatelle, you must first let the sheets dry, but only until they are slightly stiff yet completely pliable, about 30 minutes. Use a fluted pastry wheel to cut ¾–1-inch-wide ribbons for pappardelle. To make ¼-inch-wide strands for tagliatelle, run the sheet through the appropriate cutters of the pasta machine's attachment. Or, loosely roll up a sheet crosswise; cut crosswise into ¼-inch-wide strands, then unfurl.

---

## PAPPARDELLE & MUSHROOMS
### serves 4

Autumn is mushroom season in Italy's Piedmont region; markets and restaurants serve up white truffles, but it's porcini that reign as the king of mushrooms. You can use fresh porcini in this recipe in place of the cremini and dried porcini. But if you can't find fresh porcini in your market, do what we (and the Italians) do, use dried porcini with the affordable and more common cultivated cremini to add deep, earthy mushroom flavor.

*continued*

| | |
|---|---|
| 1 ounce dried porcini | 1½ pounds cremini mushrooms, sliced |
| 2 tablespoons butter | 1 cup finely chopped parsley |
| 2 tablespoons extra-virgin olive oil | Salt and pepper |
| 2 cloves garlic, minced | 1 recipe Egg Pasta (page 38) or |
| 2 tablespoons tomato paste | 1 pound dried pappardelle |

Soak the porcini in boiling water to cover, and let soften for 15 minutes. Heat the butter and oil together in a large skillet over medium-high heat. Add the garlic and sauté for 1 minute. Add the tomato paste and cook for 1 minute. Add the cremini, stir everything together, and cook for 10 minutes.

Strain the porcini, reserving the soaking liquid, and chop them. Add the porcini, their liquid, and parsley to the skillet. Season with salt and pepper. Stir to mix everything together. Cook until the sauce thickens slightly, about 2 minutes.

Cut the egg pasta into pappardelle (see page 43). Cook the pappardelle in a large pot of salted boiling water over high heat until just cooked, about 10 minutes. Drain and return to the pot, leaving behind a little of the pasta water. Add the mushroom sauce and mix everything together.

## SPINACH TAGLIATELLE
## WITH SIMPLE TOMATO SAUCE & RICOTTA

Bring a large pot of water to a boil and add 1 tablespoon salt. Heat 4–6 cups Simple Tomato Sauce (page 103) in a large skillet over medium heat until gently bubbling. Season with salt and pepper, and round out the flavors with some really good extra-virgin olive oil. Cook 1 recipe Spinach Pasta (page 38) cut into tagliatelle (page 43) or 1 pound dried tagliatelle in the boiling water until just cooked through, 2–3 minutes for fresh pasta, or 7–8 minutes for dried pasta. Drain, reserving 1 cup of the cooking water. Toss the pasta in with the tomato sauce until thoroughly coated. Stir in some of the reserved cooking water to loosen it, if you like. Divide the pasta between four plates and top with a big soup spoonful of fresh whole milk ricotta (page 102). Drizzle a little really good extra-virgin olive oil on top of each serving and grate as much parmigiano over each as you see fit. ——*serves 4*

# GNOCCHI VERDI
serves 4–6

These little dumplings have many names—gnocchi verdi, gnudi, or ravioli malfatti—but no matter what you call them, they are light and delicious.

FOR THE GNOCCHI VERDI

2 pounds fresh spinach, cooked, squeezed dry, and finely minced

1½ cups fresh whole milk ricotta (page 102)

1 tablespoon melted butter

¾ cup grated parmigiano-reggiano

2 eggs, lightly beaten

1 teaspoon nutmeg

Salt and pepper

6 tablespoons flour

FOR THE SAGE BUTTER

8–12 tablespoons butter

8–10 sage leaves

Parmigiano-reggiano

For the gnocchi verdi, mix together the spinach, ricotta, butter, parmigiano, and eggs with a rubber spatula in a large bowl. Season with nutmeg, salt, and pepper. Sift the flour through a sieve into the spinach mixture. With a spatula, mix it just enough to incorporate the flour. Overmixing the dough will make the gnocchi heavy and tough. The dough will be soft and a little sticky, that's fine. Refrigerate in a covered container for a few hours or, better still, overnight.

For the sage butter, about 20 minutes before serving, melt the butter in a small pan with the sage leaves over medium heat. Turn off heat, cover, and keep warm.

To form and cook the gnocchi, fill a wide pan with water to a depth of about 3 inches. Season with salt, and bring to a gentle simmer over medium heat. Adjust the heat to keep the water barely simmering. Have ready the chilled gnocchi dough, two teaspoons, and 1 cup cold water. Dip the spoons in the water, then scoop up some dough with one spoon. Use the other spoon to shape the gnoccho into a quenelle. Hold the spoon in the simmering water for a second and the gnocco will slide off to the bottom of the pan. Cook 6–10 gnocchi at a time. When they float to the surface, cook them for about 3 minutes.

Divide the gnocchi between flat soup bowls and spoon the warm sage butter on top. Season with salt and pepper and a shower of parmigiano.

# RICOTTA GNOCCHI
serves 4–6

We buy good-quality ricotta from our local Italian deli, but when we can't find it we make our own.

FOR THE RICOTTA GNOCCHI
2 cups fresh whole milk ricotta
  (page 102)
2 eggs, lightly beaten
1¼ cups grated parmigiano-reggiano
Grated nutmeg
Salt and pepper
1 cup flour

FOR THE SAUCE
1¼ cups Simple Tomato Sauce
  (page 103)
Salt and pepper
Really good extra-virgin olive oil
Parmigiano-reggiano

For the ricotta gnocchi, process the ricotta in a food processor until very smooth, about 2 minutes. Mix together the ricotta, eggs, and parmigiano with a rubber spatula in a large bowl. Season with nutmeg, salt, and pepper. Sift the flour through a sieve into the ricotta mixture. With a spatula, mix it just enough to incorporate the flour. Overmixing the dough will make the gnocchi heavy and tough. The dough will be soft and a little sticky, that's fine. Refrigerate it in a covered container for a few hours or, better still, overnight.

To form and cook the gnocchi, fill a wide pan with water to a depth of about 3 inches. Season with salt, and bring to a gentle simmer over medium heat. Adjust the heat to keep the water barely simmering. Have ready the chilled gnocchi dough, two teaspoons, and 1 cup cold water. Dip the spoons in the water, then scoop up some dough with one spoon. Use the other spoon to shape the gnoccho into a quenelle. Hold the spoon in the simmering water for a second and the gnoccho will slide off to the bottom of the pan. Cook 6–10 gnocchi at a time. When they float to the surface, cook them for about 3 minutes.

For the sauce, heat the tomato sauce in a small saucepan over medium heat. Spoon the sauce into flat soup bowls and top with the gnocchi. Season with salt and pepper, a drizzle of olive oil, and a shower of parmigiano.

riso

# RISOTTO BIANCO
serves 4

Risotto is traditionally made with the short-grain rice of the Po Valley. There are three main rice varieties: arborio, with its large plump grains that produce a starchy risotto; carnaroli, smaller grains that produce a looser (wavy) risotto; and vialone nano, with firm grains that cook up soft with a kernel of chewiness in the center, just the way Italians like it.

4 tablespoons butter
1 small onion, finely chopped
2 tablespoons finely chopped
   preserved lemon rind, optional

1 cup arborio, carnaroli, or vialone
   nano rice
½ cup grated parmigiano-reggiano
Salt and pepper

Fill a medium pot with about 5 cups water and bring to a gentle simmer over medium heat. Reduce heat to low and keep the water hot.

Melt 3 tablespoons of the butter in a heavy deep sauté pan over medium-high heat. Add the onions and cook, stirring with a wooden spoon, until soft and translucent, about 3 minutes. Stir the preserved lemon rind, if using, into the onions then add the rice, stirring until everything is coated with butter.

Add ½ cup of the simmering water, stirring constantly, to keep the rice from sticking to the bottom of the pan. Push any rice that crawls up the sides back down into the liquid. When the rice has absorbed all the water, add another ½ cup of water. Continue this process until you have added most of the water, about 20 minutes.

Taste the rice, it is done when it is tender with a firm center. The fully cooked risotto should be moist but not soupy. Add the parmigiano and the remaining 1 tablespoon of butter and stir until it has melted into the rice. Taste, and season with salt and pepper, if needed.

*Previous pages: left, a bag of carnaroli rice; right, top, Risotto Milanese; bottom, Risotto Bianco*

# RISOTTO MILANESE
## serves 4

Arab traders were exporting rice from Sicily as early as the tenth century, that is, 500 years before it was planted in the Po Valley, now Italy's main rice growing region. Those traders also brought traditional Arab spices to the area, saffron being one of them. Saffron imbues the rice with a golden glow—that must have thrilled the Milanese. Traditionally, marrow was added to enrich the dish, now pancetta and prosciutto stand in.

4–5 cups beef or chicken broth
½ teaspoon saffron threads
4 tablespoons butter
1 small onion, finely chopped
1 clove garlic, minced

2 tablespoons finely chopped prosciutto, optional
1 cup arborio, carnaroli, or vialone nano rice
½ cup grated parmigiano-reggiano
Salt and pepper

Heat the broth in a medium pot and bring to a gentle simmer over medium heat. Reduce the heat to low and keep the broth hot. Put the saffron in a little dish and add ½ cup of the simmering broth. Set aside to infuse.

Melt 3 tablespoons of the butter in a heavy deep sauté pan over medium-high heat. Add the onions and garlic, and cook, stirring constantly with a wooden spoon, until soft and translucent, about 3 minutes. Stir the prosciutto, if using, into the onions, then add the rice, stirring until everything is coated with butter.

Add ½ cup of the simmering broth, stirring constantly to keep the rice from sticking to the bottom of the pan. Push any rice that crawls up the sides of the pan back down into the liquid. When the rice has absorbed all the broth, add another ½ cup of simmering broth. Continue this process until you have added half of the broth, about 20 minutes, then add the saffron-infused broth.

Keep adding broth and stirring. Taste the rice, it is done when it is tender with a firm center. The fully cooked risotto should be moist but not soupy. Add the parmigiano and the remaining 1 tablespoon of butter, and stir until it has melted into the rice. Taste, and season with salt and pepper, if needed.

# RISOTTO ALLA CERTOSINA
## serves 4

This is our take on a risotto from Certosa di Pavia, a fifteenth-century monastery in the center of Lombardy's rice region. Carthusian monks, the very same religious order that created the herb-based liqueur Chartreuse, lived a life of self-sufficiency. They used whatever was around them: rice and the things they found in the watery fields—frogs, small fish, and crayfish. We simplified, it just seemed right.

1 pound shrimp
4 tablespoons butter
1 tablespoon extra-virgin olive oil
2 small onions, finely chopped
1 rib celery, finely chopped
1 carrot, finely chopped
1 clove garlic, sliced

Handful of parsley stems, chopped
Salt and pepper
One 14-ounce can crushed tomatoes
⅔ cup dry vermouth
Peel of 1 lemon
1 cup arborio, carnaroli, or
    vialone nano rice

Peel and devein the shrimp, reserving the shells for the broth, and set aside. Melt 1 tablespoon of the butter with the olive oil in a large pot over medium-high heat. Add the shrimp shells, half of the onions, the celery, carrots, garlic, and parsley stems. Season with salt and pepper, and sauté until golden, about 10 minutes. Add the tomatoes, ⅓ cup of the vermouth, and lemon peel, and cook for 5 minutes. Add 4 cups water and cook for 15 minutes. Strain the broth, then return it to the pot. Add the shrimp and place the pot on the stove, off the heat.

Melt 2 tablespoons of the butter in a heavy deep sauté pan over medium-high heat. Add the remaining onions and cook, stirring constantly with a wooden spoon, until soft and translucent, about 3 minutes. Add the rice, stirring until it is coated with butter. Add the remaining ⅓ cup vermouth.

Add ½ cup of the hot broth, stirring constantly to keep the rice from sticking to the bottom of the pan. Push any rice that crawls up the sides of the pan back down into the liquid. When the rice has absorbed all the broth, add another ½ cup of simmering broth. Keep adding broth and stirring. Taste the rice, it is done when it is tender with a firm center. Add the shrimp and the remaining 1 tablespoon of butter and stir until it has melted into the rice.

# TUMMALA DI RISOTTO E SPINACI
## serves 4–6

My friend and I arrived in a remote Sicilian mountain village late one autumn afternoon. We checked into rooms in an ancient crumbling palazzo just outside the village. Rather unnervingly, we were the only guests. We joined the patrician owners for dinner in the empty cavernous dining room while a tempest raged outside. The scene and vibe were lugubrious. We had just finished the antipasti when there was a loud banging on the door. No one made a move—doors aren't opened in the dark of night. Finally, a very old butler shuffled across the room and cautiously opened the heavy door a tiny crack—in pushed six rain-soaked, hopelessly lost, boisterous Germans. Greeted with suspicion, they were begrudgingly shown to a table. Soon wine was flowing and songs were being sung—they lifted the mood. But while we feasted on a sumptuous *tummala*, they were served fried eggs. —— CH

| | |
|---|---|
| 3 tablespoons extra-virgin olive oil, plus some for greasing the mold | 1 cup fresh spinach, cooked, squeezed dry, and finely minced |
| ¼ cup dried bread crumbs | 1 cup grated pecorino |
| 2 cloves garlic, finely chopped | 2 eggs, lightly beaten |
| ¼ teaspoon crushed red pepper flakes | ½ whole nutmeg, grated |
| ½ pound bulk sweet Italian sausage | Salt and pepper |
| 3 cups chopped roast chicken | 3 cups cold Risotto Bianco (page 52) |

Generously grease the inside of a 9-cup bowl or mold with oil. Dust the mold with bread crumbs, reserving some for the top. Heat the oil in a medium pan over medium-high heat, add the garlic, and cook until soft, about 2 minutes. Add the red pepper flakes and sausage. Break up the sausage with a wooden spoon and cook until crumbly and no longer pink, about 10 minutes. Transfer to a large mixing bowl and allow to cool slightly. Add the chicken, spinach, pecorino, eggs, nutmeg, and salt and pepper, and mix the filling together.

Preheat oven to 375°. Press the rice into the bottom and up the sides of the mold, using the back of a large spoon, and reserve some for the top. Fill the mold with the filling, pressing with the spoon to pack it all in. Cover with the remaining rice. Brush with oil and sprinkle with bread crumbs. Bake for 1 hour.

Run a thin-bladed knife between the mold and rice, unmold on a plate, and serve.

*Fishermen in Livorno*

# STEWED EEL
## serves 8

Eel begins appearing in Italian markets right before Christmas. We order ours from our fishmonger. We realize that a recipe starting with the instructions "Cut off the head" could make you squeamish. If that's the case, just ask your fishmonger to do "the dirty work" for you.

1 whole eel, about 4 pounds, cleaned

Salt and pepper

2 cups flour

2 cups olive oil

¾ cup red wine vinegar

1 medium onion, chopped

2 tablespoons tomato paste

Pinch of crushed red pepper flakes

1 cup Simple Tomato Sauce (page 103)

Cut off the head, 2 inches of the tail, and the wings running along the top and bottom of the eel. Cut the eel crosswise into pieces about 2 inches thick. Season the eel with salt and pepper and dredge in flour, shaking off any excess.

Heat 1½ cups of the olive oil in a large, wide, enameled cast-iron or other heavy pot over medium-high heat. Working in batches, lightly brown the eel on both sides, about 10 minutes. Transfer the eel to paper towels. Discard the oil, wipe out the pot, and set aside.

Bring the vinegar and 4 cups water to a simmer in a medium saucepan. Meanwhile, heat the remaining ½ cup of oil in the large pot over medium-high heat. Add the onions and cook, stirring often, until lightly browned, 5–10 minutes. Stir in the tomato paste and cook for 1 minute. Add the pepper flakes. Add about half of the vinegar water, scraping up any brown bits stuck to the bottom of the pot. Add the tomato sauce and bring to a simmer.

Return the eel to the pot. Cook the eel, giving the sauce a stir and basting the eel frequently, until the sauce is thick and smooth and the eel is tender and the flesh pulls away from the bone easily, about 10 minutes. If the sauce gets too thick, thin it with the vinegar water. Season with salt and pepper.

# OIL-POACHED SWORDFISH
## serves 2–4

I had some grocery shopping to do one morning before heading to the studio at Canal House, so I hit our local ShopRite, grabbed a cart, picked up some focaccia at the bakery, and was on the way to the meat department when I came to a stop. Two aproned, muscular guys in white T-shirts were standing behind the cheese counter, one working a long wooden paddle in a big vat of warm milk, stirring and lifting, while the other stretched and shaped fresh curds into fat wet balls of mozzarella, right there in the *supermarket!* (Somehow I'd never caught them before on their two cheese-making days.) I bought four warm balls—how could I resist?

Moving on to the meat department, I passed the onions and garlic in produce and had to stop again. There, in the middle of the aisle, was a whole swordfish, the size of me, displayed on ice. Packages of thick, beautiful, pink-tinged swordfish steaks were neatly arranged alongside the fish. I was beginning to feel like I was in Italy! A handwritten sign: "Special $12.99/lb. Line-caught off the Jersey Shore" reeled me all the way in. As I put two of the steaks in my cart, another customer looked on, first at the fish, then at me, and asked how to cook it. "Oh, it's easy," I said. "You can grill it, or broil it, or pan fry it." Unconvinced, she pushed on, looking a little frightened. Her loss.

Back at Canal House, we sliced the warm cheese, drizzled it with olive oil, and had it on toast for breakfast. And the swordfish? We decided to poach it in oil, like we often do with fresh tuna. Not a bad catch for the day's lunch! ——MH

1 thick, center-cut loin swordfish
   steak, about 1 pound
4 cups extra-virgin olive oil
Zest of 1 lemon, cut in wide strips

12 black peppercorns
2 cloves garlic, halved
1 small dried red chile
1 bay leaf

Put the swordfish in a medium pan and cover it with oil. Add the zest, peppercorns, garlic, chile, and bay leaf. Gently poach the fish over low heat until opaque and just cooked through, 20–30 minutes. Serve warm or at room temperature, divided into large pieces, with a spoonful of the oil, some salt, and warm crusty bread, if you like, to sop up the oil and juices on the plates.

# SALT COD WITH TOMATOES & GREEN OLIVES
serves 4–8

I was raised in a big Irish Catholic family and while there were lots of holidays and feast days to celebrate, there wasn't much to feast on (save Saint
Patrick's Day corned beef and cabbage). Lucky for us, Aunt Frances fell in
love and married an Italian, our Uncle Fred. He made wine in his base-
ment, ravioli so delicate they melted in your mouth, and *baccalà* on Christmas Eve for La Vigilia, The Feast of the Seven Fishes. Although I don't
have a drop of Italian blood in my veins, I feel like a *paisan* and remember
my lovely uncle whenever I make this dish. —— CH

2 pounds salt cod
½ cup extra-virgin olive oil, plus
   more for the bread
2 cloves garlic, thinly sliced
1 onion, thinly sliced
¼ teaspoon crushed red pepper flakes
20 pitted Cerignola olives, chopped

½ cup oil-packed sun-dried tomatoes,
   finely chopped
Grated zest of 1–2 large lemons
1 cup Simple Tomato Sauce
   (page 103)
½ cup packed chopped fresh parsley
12 slices country bread

Soak the salt cod in a bowl of water for 24 hours, changing the water several
times. Drain and rinse. Cut the fish into same size pieces. Remove any skin and
check for and remove any bones. Put the fish in a large pan, cover with cold
water, and bring just to a boil over high heat. Reduce heat to low and barely
simmer for 20 minutes. Use a slotted spatula to transfer the fish to a paper
towel-lined plate to cool. When cool enough to handle, break into large flakes.

Dry the same pan, add the oil, and heat over medium heat. Add the garlic,
onions, and pepper flakes, and cook until soft, 5 minutes. Add the olives, sun-
dried tomatoes, and lemon zest, and stir everything together. Add the tomato
sauce and 1 cup water. Add the salt cod, taking care not to break it up too
much, and simmer until the sauce thickens slightly, about 10 minutes. Reduce
the heat to low, and gently simmer for 20 minutes. Add the parsley.

Preheat the oven to 400°. Brush the bread with olive oil on both sides and
arrange in a single layer on a baking sheet. Toast the bread in the oven until
golden, about 3 minutes, then turn and toast the other side. Serve with the
warm salt cod.

# BRANZINO WITH SHRIMP & FENNEL
### serves 4

Branzino is a Mediterranean sea bass that swims in the waters all around the boot of Italy. When it swims over to France, the French call this fish *loup de mer*. The Italians and Greeks are farm-raising branzino organically, so look for that. We like to buy whole fish, that way it's easy to see how fresh it is by looking it straight in the eye (which should be bright and clear, never cloudy). We ask our fishmonger to butterfly and debone the fish, but keep the head and tail attached, so the body of the fish opens up like a book. Really, any white-fleshed fish would be a delicious substitute.

1 pound small shrimp, peeled and deveined

1 cup minced fennel bulb, plus some chopped fronds for garnish

2 tablespoons extra-virgin olive oil

Juice and zest of 1 lemon

1 tablespoon ground fennel seeds

½ tablespoon freshly ground pepper

Salt

2 whole branzino, butterflied and deboned, with the head and tail attached

Really good extra-virgin olive oil

1 lemon, cut into wedges

Preheat the oven to 500°. Mix together the shrimp, fennel bulb, olive oil, lemon juice and zest, ground fennel seeds, pepper, and salt to taste in a mixing bowl. You can make this a few hours ahead (in fact, it will benefit from it) and refrigerate until ready to cook.

Line 2 baking sheets with parchment paper and place each branzino, open like a book, skin side down on the paper. Divide the shrimp evenly between the fish, arranging them on top of each one. Spoon the marinade over the shrimp.

Cook in the oven until the shrimp and the fish are opaque, about 20 minutes. Remove from the oven and transfer the fish to a large warm platter. Drizzle with really good extra-virgin olive oil, and garnish with fennel fronds and lemon wedges. For individual servings, divide each fish into 2 filets and place them on 4 plates, with the shrimp on top. Drizzle with really good extra-virgin olive oil and serve garnished with fennel fronds and lemon wedges.

# SQUID & POTATOES
## serves 4

Grilled squid may conjure up images of Sardinia's sun-drenched Costa Smeralda for some, but it's a dish we prepare all year long. The Franklin wood-burning stove at the Canal House studio is outfitted with a removable grill that swivels and cantilevers over the fire, so when it gets cold outside, we grill inside, over wood coals. Patty Curtan, our Northern California friend, the exquisite printer, designer, and wonderful cook, grills tender squid from nearby Monterey Bay outside on her Tuscan grill. It's from her that we learned the art of skewering squid. Instead of using two skewers to keep the squid from spinning around when they're turned over, she just threads each one crosswise through the wide top of the body, lining them up on the same skewer like laundry drying on a clothesline. Leave it to Patty—so logical, so simple, so beautifully done.

2 pounds cleaned squid
1½ cups extra-virgin olive oil
4 cloves garlic, thinly sliced
Big pinch of crushed red pepper flakes
Salt and pepper

1 onion, halved and sliced lengthwise
2 russet potatoes, peeled and cut crosswise into ¼-inch-thick slices
1 lemon, quartered

Lay the squid in a dish and add 1 cup of the oil, half the garlic, the red pepper flakes, and some salt and pepper. Cover and marinate at room temperature for at least 1 hour and up to 8 hours in the refrigerator.

Put the remaining ½ cup of oil in a large skillet over medium heat. Add the onions and the remaining garlic, and arrange the potatoes on top. Pour ½ cup water over the potatoes and season with salt and pepper. Cover and cook until the onions are soft and the potatoes are tender, about 30 minutes.

Prepare a hot charcoal grill. Thread the squid bodies onto metal or wood skewers about an inch from the top and the tentacles similarly through the round body end. Grill the squid over hot coals until opaque and well marked on each side, about 5 minutes. Discard the marinade.

Put the onions and potatoes on a serving platter. Slide the squid off the skewers and arrange them on top. Drizzle a little oil over the squid, season with salt, and serve with lemon wedges.

big birds

little rabbit

# ROAST CAPON WITH DRESSING
### serves 6–8

We stay true to Thanksgiving and serve turkey, but for Christmas we love to roast big, juicy capons like the Italians do. For large gatherings, we roast a few, stuffing each one with a different dressing.

1 capon or roasting hen,
  6–9 pounds
3 tablespoons butter, softened

Salt and pepper
5–8 cups dressing (recipes follow)
Fresh sage, optional

Preheat the oven to 350°. Rub the capon all over with butter and season it inside and out with salt and pepper. Spoon the dressing into the cavity. Tie the legs together with kitchen string.

Put the capon on a rack set inside a large roasting pan, and add 1 cup water. Roast the capon, basting it occasionally with pan juices, until it is golden brown and the internal temperature of the thigh meat registers 165°, about 2 hours.

Let the capon rest for about 20 minutes before carving it. Serve the capon and pan juices with the dressing on a large serving platter, and garnish with fresh sage, if you like.

# CHESTNUTS, PRUNES & BREAD CRUMBS
### makes about 8 cups

Although prepared peeled chestnuts, the ones that come vacuum-packed or in jars, are already cooked and reasonably tender, their flavor and texture benefit from a bit of time simmering in hot liquid—in this case, sweet wine.

1½ cups vin santo or Marsala
4 cups peeled whole chestnuts,
  vacuum-packed or in a jar
1½ cups pitted prunes, halved
8 tablespoons butter

8 ounces pancetta, diced
1 medium onion, finely chopped
5 cups coarse, fresh bread crumbs
½ bunch parsley, leaves chopped
Salt and pepper

Put the wine and chestnuts into a medium saucepan and simmer over medium-low heat for 15 minutes. Add the prunes and set aside to cool.

Meanwhile, melt the butter in a large skillet over medium-high heat. Add the pancetta and onions and cook, stirring often, until the onions are soft, about 5 minutes. Add the bread crumbs, reduce the heat to medium, and cook, stirring often, until golden, about 10 minutes. Remove the skillet from the heat. Using a slotted spoon, add the chestnuts and prunes to the skillet. Add the parsley and season generously with salt and pepper. Mix the dressing together, stirring in just enough of the wine to moisten without it becoming packed or dense.

Spoon the dressing into the capon cavity and roast. Put any extra dressing into a buttered ovenproof dish, cover, and bake in a 350° oven until hot, 20–30 minutes. Uncover and bake until golden on top, about 20 minutes.

## SAUSAGE & APPLES
makes about 6 cups

4 tablespoons butter
1 onion, chopped
1 rib celery, chopped
¼ teaspoon fennel seeds
1 pound sweet Italian sausage,
   removed from casings

½ bunch parsley, leaves chopped
2–4 fresh sage leaves, chopped
Salt and pepper
3–4 cups fresh bread crumbs
1 apple, peeled, cored, and diced
½ cup chicken stock

Melt the butter in a large skillet over medium heat. Add the onions, celery, and fennel seeds, and cook, stirring occasionally, until soft, about 5 minutes. Add the sausage and cook, breaking it up with the back of a spoon, until it is no longer pink, about 5 minutes. Stir in the herbs and generously season with salt and pepper. Transfer to a large bowl. Add the bread crumbs and apples and toss until well combined. Stir in the stock, mixing until the dressing is moist but not packed or dense. Adjust the seasonings.

Spoon the dressing into the capon cavity and roast. Put any extra dressing into a buttered ovenproof dish, cover, and bake in a 350° oven until hot, 20–30 minutes. Uncover and bake until golden on top, about 20 minutes.

*Overleaf: Roast Capon with Dressing*

## POACHED CAPON IN RICH BRODO
serves 6–8

Christmas is the capon's time to sing. They are a bit expensive and a large roasting hen can stand in for the castrated rooster. Cluck, cluck, cluck!

1 capon, 6–9 pounds
4 carrots, coarsely chopped
4 ribs celery, coarsely chopped
2 medium onions, chopped

1 small bunch fresh parsley
1 tablespoon black peppercorns
Salt
Parmigiano-reggiano

Remove the breast from the capon, making 2 boneless breast halves, and set aside. Cut up the remaining bird into 8 pieces and put them into a heavy large pot over medium heat. Cover and cook, stirring occasionally, until some of the fat and juices have been released, 15–20 minutes. Add the carrots, celery, onions, parsley, peppercorns, and 6 quarts cold water. Bring to a boil over high heat, skimming any foam. Reduce the heat to medium-low. Add the breasts and poach until just tender, 20–30 minutes. Transfer the breasts to a plate. Remove and discard the skin. Cover the meat and refrigerate. Continue simmering the broth until the dark meat is tender, about 1 hour.

Strain the broth through a fine-mesh strainer into a large bowl. Pull out the thighs and drumsticks, separate the meat from the bones, discarding the bones and skin. Cover and refrigerate the meat. Strain the broth a second time into a large clean pot, leaving any debris behind. Boil the broth over medium-high heat until reduced by about half (12–14 cups), about 1 hour. Season with salt.

Thickly slice the breasts and add to the broth along with the reserved dark meat and warm through over low heat. Serve the capon and broth in warm wide soup bowls. Grate as much parmigiano into the bowls as you like.

COLD CAPON SALAD: Put the slices of poached capon breast and dark meat into a glass or ceramic dish. Add ½ cup really good extra-virgin olive oil, juice of 1 lemon, 2 tablespoons white wine vinegar, ¼ cup golden raisins, 2 tablespoons capers, a large pinch of crushed red pepper flakes, and 1 teaspoon sugar. Season with salt and pepper and gently mix everything together. Cover and refrigerate overnight. Bring to room temperature before serving with a salad of endive and arugula. —— *serves 4*

# ROAST GUINEA HEN WITH CIPOLLINE & CHESTNUTS
## serves 4

It had been drizzling all morning on a late autumn day as we drove through the hills of the Piedmont up toward the mountains of the Valle d'Aosta. By early afternoon we were hungry and ready to stop for lunch. It's every traveler's dilemma, "Where should we eat?" It's hard to size up a restaurant at a glance. But on this day we chose right; the inside lived up to its charming facade. As we stepped through the door, we were warmly greeted, then led to a table next to the fireplace. We started with bagna cauda, then we both chose this dish made with the region's red wine and chestnuts—it tasted like nowhere else.

1 guinea hen, cut into 4 pieces (legs and breasts)
Salt and pepper
½ teaspoon cinnamon
3 tablespoons extra-virgin olive oil
4 ounces pancetta, diced

12 cipolline, peeled
24 peeled whole chestnuts, vacuum-packed or in a jar
1 cup red wine
1 cup rich poultry broth

Season the guinea hen with salt, pepper, and cinnamon, and set aside.

Heat the olive oil in a large skillet over medium-high heat. Add the pancetta, cipolline, and chestnuts, and sauté until the cipolline are golden, about 10 minutes. Use a slotted spatula to transfer everything to a platter and set side. Leave the oil in the skillet.

Add the guinea hen to the skillet and sauté, turning the pieces several times, until they are golden on all sides, 5–10 minutes. Transfer to the platter. Increase the heat to high, add the wine, and cook until reduced to about ½ cup. Add the broth to the skillet and bring to a boil. Reduce the heat to medium and return the guinea hen legs to the skillet, then spoon the pancetta, cipolline, and chestnuts on top. Cover and cook for 30 minutes.

Add the breasts to the skillet, cover, and cook for 15 minutes. Transfer the guinea hen to a platter, then spoon the pancetta, cipolline, and chestnuts on top. Increase the heat to high and reduce the sauce until it thickens slightly, about 2 minutes. Pour the sauce over the guinea hen and serve.

## BRAISED RABBIT WITH CAPERS & PANCETTA
serves 4

This dish, based on one we ate in Puglia, gets its balanced depth of saltiness from anchovies and capers, two ingredients we often favor in place of salt. We couldn't resist adding chewy pancetta.

1 rabbit, 3 pounds
3 tablespoons extra-virgin olive oil
4 ounces pancetta, diced
2 carrots, peeled and diced
1 medium onion, chopped
1 rib celery, diced

1 bay leaf
2 cups dry white wine
¼ cup red or white wine vinegar
6 anchovy filets, minced
2 tablespoons capers
Pepper

Lay the rabbit on its back. Using a sharp knife, cut off the hind legs at the joint near the backbone. Cut under the shoulder blades to remove the forelegs from the rib cage. Trim off the rib cage on either side of the loin, then trim off the neck and tail ends of the loin. Save the rib cage and end pieces for another use, or discard. Cut the loin crosswise, through the backbone, in two or three pieces. Set the rabbit aside.

Heat 2 tablespoons of the oil in a heavy medium pot over medium heat. Add the pancetta and cook, stirring occasionally, until lightly browned, about 10 minutes. Use a slotted spoon to transfer the pancetta to a small plate and set aside. Add the remaining 1 tablespoon of oil to the pot. Add the rabbit and lightly brown all over, 8–10 minutes. Transfer to a plate and set aside.

Add the carrots, onions, celery, and bay leaf to the pot and cook, stirring often, until the vegetables begin to soften, 5–10 minutes. Stir in the wine and vinegar, scraping up any browned bits stuck to the bottom of the pot with a wooden spoon. Return the rabbit and pancetta to the pot.

Cover the pot, reduce the heat to medium-low, and braise the rabbit until it is just cooked through and tender but not dry, about 30 minutes. Uncover the pot. Add the anchovies and capers and simmer until the sauce thickens slightly, about 5 minutes. Remove the bay leaf. Season with pepper.

# CABBAGE & FENNEL WITH SAUSAGES & BORLOTTI
## serves 4–8

If you cook the beans ahead, this Sardinian peasant dish can be on the table in a little more than half an hour.

½ pound dried borlotti or cranberry beans

4 cloves garlic, crushed and peeled

Salt and pepper

6 tablespoons extra-virgin olive oil

4–8 small Italian sausages

1 onion, finely chopped

¼ teaspoon crushed red pepper flakes

1–2 teaspoons ground fennel seeds

1 fennel bulb, finely chopped

2 tablespoons tomato paste

½ cup red wine

1 cup canned whole plum tomatoes

1 pound Savoy cabbage, sliced

Put the beans in a medium pot and cover with cold water by at least 2 inches. Add 2 of the garlic cloves to the pot. Bring to a boil over medium-high heat. Cover, turn off the heat, and allow to soak for 1 hour. Turn the heat on to medium-high, bring to a boil, then reduce the heat to low. Cover and barely simmer until the beans are tender, 1–1½ hours. The fresher the beans the more quickly they will cook. Don't drain. Season with salt and pepper and 3 tablespoons of the olive oil. Cook the beans up to 3 days ahead.

Heat the remaining 3 tablespoons of oil in a heavy deep large skillet over medium-high heat. Add the sausages and prick them all over with a fork. Cook, turning the sausages until they are browned all over, about 10 minutes. Remove the sausages from the skillet, and set aside.

Add the remaining 2 cloves of garlic, onions, red pepper flakes, and ground fennel seeds. Cook, stirring every now and then, until the onions are soft, about 5 minutes. Add the chopped fennel bulb, then stir in the tomato paste, and continue to cook for about 2 minutes. Increase the heat to high, add the wine, and cook until reduced by half and the vegetables absorb most of it, about 2 minutes. Add the tomatoes and stir until they dissolve into the sauce.

Reduce the heat to medium, add the cabbage and the sausages, cover, and cook until the cabbage is tender, about 15 minutes. Season with salt and pepper. Serve in soup plates with big spoonfuls of beans.

*Previous pages: left, Pino Cinquemani; right, with his butchers in front of Pino Prime Meats, NYC*

# BRAISED LAMB & GREEN BEANS
serves 4

Look for whole San Marzano plum tomatoes in cans, imported from Italy. They are worth the hunt. Full of flavor, they have tender meaty flesh that melts into sauces. Italians like their vegetables thoroughly cooked—they may like their pasta *al dente*, but not their green beans.

| | |
|---|---|
| 3 tablespoons extra-virgin olive oil | 3 cloves garlic, sliced |
| ¼ teaspoon crushed red pepper flakes | ½ cup red wine |
| 2 pounds lamb shoulder, cut into 2-inch pieces | 3 small branches fresh rosemary |
| | 1–2 pounds green beans, trimmed |
| Salt and pepper | 1 cup canned whole plum tomatoes |
| 4 anchovy filets | |

Heat the olive oil in a heavy large skillet with a lid over medium-high heat. Add the pepper flakes. Add the lamb and season it with salt and pepper. Brown the lamb in 2 batches, transferring the cooked lamb from the skillet to a platter.

Add the anchovies to the skillet and stir with a wooden spoon until they have melted into the oil. Add the garlic, and stir for a minute. Return the lamb and any accumulated juices to the skillet. Add the wine and tuck the rosemary around the lamb. Reduce the heat to low, cover, and slowly simmer the lamb until tender, about 1 hour.

While the lamb cooks, put the beans in a medium pot with about 1 cup water. Cover and cook over medium heat until very well done, 15–20 minutes. Drain and season with salt and pepper.

When the lamb is tender, remove the rosemary. Add the crushed tomatoes and stir them into the sauce until the tomatoes dissolve. Cook until the sauce thickens slightly. Serve the lamb and its sauce over the green beans.

# MEATBALLS WITH MINT & PARSLEY
## makes about 24

We serve platters of these tender meatballs along with broccoli rabe
sautéed with garlic and crushed red pepper flakes.

1 pound ground pork
1 pound ground veal
¼ pound prosciutto, finely chopped
1 cup fresh whole milk ricotta
  (page 102)
1 cup grated pecorino
2 eggs
¼ cup packed finely chopped fresh
  mint leaves

¼ cup packed finely chopped fresh
  parsley leaves
½ whole nutmeg, grated
Pepper
¼ cup extra-virgin olive oil
½ cup white wine
¾ cup heavy cream, optional
Salt

Mix together the pork, veal, prosciutto, ricotta, pecorino, eggs, mint, parsley,
nutmeg, and pepper in a large mixing bowl.

Use a large soupspoon and scoop up about 2 ounces of the meat into your
hand and roll into a ball. Make all the meatballs the same size so they will
cook evenly. As you make them, arrange them in a single layer on a baking
sheet. You can do this a few hours ahead, cover with plastic, and refrigerate
until you are ready to cook them.

Heat 2 tablespoons of the oil in a heavy large skillet over medium-high
heat. Brown the meatballs in batches, about 15 minutes per batch, using
two forks to delicately turn them over so that they brown on all sides. Add
more oil, if needed. Transfer the cooked meatballs to a platter and cover
with foil to keep them warm.

Increase the heat to high and deglaze the skillet with the wine, stirring
with a wooden spoon to loosen any browned bits stuck to the bottom
of the skillet. Add the cream, if using, and cook, stirring, until the sauce
thickens. Taste, then season with salt, if necessary. Pour the sauce through
a fine-mesh sieve over the meatballs and serve.

*Overleaf: left, Meatballs with Mint & Parsley; right, a specialty food shop in the pretty Piedmont town of Alba*

# OSSO BUCO
## serves 8

This has been a New Year's Eve favorite of ours for years. We serve it with Risotto Milanese (page 53), the soft rich marrow from the bones enriching the golden saffron rice. On less celebratory occasions, we serve them with toothsome polenta or wide egg noodles.

8 veal shanks, 2 inches thick, tied with kitchen string

Salt and pepper

6 tablespoons olive oil

4 tablespoons butter

3 medium carrots, diced

3 ribs celery, diced

2 medium onions, diced

2 cups dry white wine

One 28-ounce can whole peeled plum tomatoes in juice

2–3 cups chicken or veal stock

2 bay leaves

1 handful fresh parsley leaves, finely chopped

Grated zest of 1 large lemon

2 small cloves garlic, minced

Preheat the oven to 350°. Season the shanks with salt and pepper. Heat the oil in a heavy large pot with a lid over medium-high heat. Working in batches, brown the shanks, 8–10 minutes per side. Transfer them to a large plate as they brown. Wipe the oil and blackened bits out of the pot.

Return the pot to medium heat, melt the butter, add the carrots, celery, and onions, and cook until softened, 15–20 minutes. Stir in the wine. Return the shanks and any accumulated juices to the pot, nestling them in layers. Add the tomatoes, crushing them with your hands as you drop them in the pot. Pour in enough stock to nearly cover the shanks, adding a little water, if necessary. Season with salt and pepper and tuck in the bay leaves.

Cover the pot and braise the shanks in the oven, basting them halfway through, until very tender (the meat should almost fall off the bone, but the string holds it in place), 2–2½ hours. Discard the bay leaves.

For the gremolata, combine the parsley, lemon zest, and garlic in a small bowl.

Serve the osso buco with the chunky sauce as is, or pass it through a sieve, pressing the vegetables through. Add a small spoonful of gremolata to the top of each marrow bone.

# NEW YEAR'S COTECHINO WITH LENTILS
## serves 8

We've found packaged cotechino at our local Italian grocery store, but the best ones come from the Italian butcher shops that still make their own version of this fresh pork sausage, a specialty of Emilia-Romagna. It may be unorthodox, but we prepare this classic New Year's dish with the tiny brown lentils from Umbria because they keep their dainty shape when cooked.

2 cotechino sausages, about
  1 pound each
3 tablespoons extra-virgin olive oil
1 onion, very finely diced
1 carrot, very finely diced
1 rib celery, very finely diced
1 garlic clove, minced
½ teaspoon nutmeg

Pinch of crushed red pepper flakes
1 bay leaf
1 pound lentils (preferably from
  Umbria), rinsed
Salt and pepper
1 bunch parsley, leaves chopped
Really good extra-virgin olive oil

Put the sausages into a deep, wide pot with plenty of room, then cover with 2–3 inches of water. Bring to a boil. Reduce the heat to medium-low and cover the pot. Poach the sausages until they are heated through (or to an internal temperature of about 160°), about 1 hour. Turn off the heat.

Heat the olive oil in a medium pot over medium heat until warm. Add the onions, carrots, and celery, and cook until the onions are translucent, about 5 minutes. Stir in the garlic, nutmeg, red pepper flakes, and bay leaf, and cook until fragrant, about 1 minute. Add the lentils and 5–6 cups of the cotechino poaching liquid. Bring to a simmer. Reduce the heat to medium-low, cover, and simmer until the lentils are tender, 20–30 minutes. Add a little more liquid to the lentils as they cook, if necessary. Season with salt and pepper.

Remove the cotechino from the liquid, peel off the casing, and thickly slice. Using a slotted spoon, put the lentils on a serving platter, discarding the bay leaf and extra liquid. Scatter the parsley on top and drizzle with the really good extra-virgin olive oil. Arrange the sliced cotechino on top.

eat your verdure

## PORCINI IN UMIDO

If you've followed our series of seasonal recipes since the beginning, you probably know about our love for wild mushrooms, especially for chanterelles—*Cantharellus cibarius,* the golden beauties we gather in our neck of the woods. But it's no wonder that most people consider the king of them all to be the porcini, *Boletus edulis,* one we rarely find in our woods, and certainly not as often as we'd like in our markets. It rivals truffles with its perfume and rich meaty texture. The Italians know how to leave a good thing alone and this simple preparation is all this mushroom needs.

Warm ½ cup extra-virgin olive oil and 2–3 cloves thinly sliced garlic together in a large skillet over medium-low to medium heat until fragrant. Add 1 pound thickly sliced, cleaned, fresh porcini. Season with salt and pepper. Cover and stew the mushrooms until they are tender, 10–20 minutes. Add a handful of chopped fresh parsley. Serve over thick slices of warm crusty toast. —— *serves 4*

## CABBAGE IN AGRODOLCE

*Agrodolce* is a classic Sicilian "sweet and sour" sauce—in fact, that is the very meaning of the name. We serve this piquant cabbage with roasted birds and meat in the fall and winter.

Heat 3 tablespoons extra-virgin olive oil in a skillet over medium heat. Add 2 thinly sliced garlic cloves, ¼ teaspoon crushed red pepper flakes, and ¼ cup minced prosciutto, and cook for about 2 minutes. Add ½ cup currants and ½ cup red wine and cook until the currants plump up and the wine reduces. Add ⅓–½ cup good-quality red wine vinegar, ¼ cup tomato sauce, and ½ cup water and stir everything together. Add 1 trimmed and thickly shredded small Savoy or green cabbage and stir to coat the leaves with the sauce. Cover and cook, stirring occasionally, until the cabbage is tender, about 25 minutes. Taste to see if the flavor is balanced, then season with salt and pepper. —— *serves 4*

*Previous pages: left, porcini; right, a mushroom seller in the Mercato di Sant'Ambrogio, Florence*

# STUFFED ONIONS PIEDMONTESE
## makes 8

Stuffed onions are a specialty of the Piedmont region. Traditionally, a little ground veal is added to the stuffing, but we use prosciutto instead, which we always keep on hand. Boneless prosciutto shanks are sold at our local Italian grocery store and they are perfect for chopping or dicing. We also like the way they add meaty flavor and subtle saltiness. Or you can add diced pancetta instead. Use this bread crumb recipe to stuff peppers, tomatoes, zucchini, or any other vegetable that you like.

4 onions, peeled and halved crosswise
1 cup fresh bread crumbs
2 cloves garlic, sliced
¼ cup finely chopped prosciutto
¼ cup loosely packed fresh
   parsley leaves

½ teaspoon fresh rosemary leaves
½ cup grated parmigiano-reggiano
Salt and pepper
¼ cup extra-virgin olive oil

Put the onions cut side up in a pan and add enough water to cover them. Bring to a gentle boil over medium heat, cover, reduce heat to low, and cook for 10 minutes. Use a slotted spatula to transfer them from the pan to a paper towel-lined plate to drain. When the onions are cool enough to handle, remove the 2–4 center rings, leaving thick-walled "onion cups" for stuffing.

Put the onion centers, bread crumbs, garlic, prosciutto, parsley, rosemary, and parmigiano in the bowl of a food processor and pulse to finely chop and mix everything together. Season to taste with salt and pepper.

Preheat the oven to 350°. Pour a little of the olive oil in the bottom of a large baking dish. Arrange the onion cups in the dish and spoon the filling into the onions, packing it down with the back of a spoon. Mound any extra on top of each onion. Drizzle the onions with the remaining olive oil.

Bake the onions, basting them occasionally, until they are tender, about 1 hour. Serve them hot or at room temperature.

## PEPPERS IN AGRODOLCE
### makes 8 peppers

Look for meaty red peppers with an elongated shape, we think they're prettier. Our agrodolce is a balance of sweet and sour—currants and aged balsamic vinegar—with anchovies adding a mysterious salty flavor. There is a luscious sensuality to these peppers. We make a double recipe and keep them on hand to drape over quickly grilled fish, meat, or poultry; an easy way to dress up an everyday meal.

1 cup currants
2–4 tablespoons aged balsamic
    vinegar
8 large, long red bell peppers

8 anchovy filets
Salt and pepper
Really good extra-virgin olive oil
Fresh basil leaves, optional

Put the currants in a cup and add ¾ cup boiling water and the vinegar, cover, and set aside to macerate for about 1 hour.

Char the peppers by placing them directly on the burners of a gas stove, or on a grill, with the flame turned up high. Use tongs to turn the peppers so their skin blackens on all sides. Or roast them in a preheated 450° oven on a baking sheet, turning several times, for about 30 minutes. Place in a plastic bag and allow the peppers to steam. When the peppers have cooled, peel off the blackened skin. Cut off the stem ends, slit open the peppers on one side and remove the seeds. Don't rinse the peppers, it will wash away their smoky flavor.

Slip 1 anchovy filet inside each pepper. Arrange the peppers in a container with a cover. Season with salt and pepper. Strain the currant soaking water into a small pot and reduce over high heat to about ¼ cup. Pour over the peppers. Scatter the currants over the peppers. Then add enough olive oil to just cover. Serve garnished with basil leaves, if you like. Refrigerate peppers, covered, for up to 1 week.

# CHICKPEAS WITH STEWED TOMATOES
serves 6–8

Look for the "best used by" date when buying a bag of chickpeas. The fresher the beans, the more quickly they will cook. They really need a good soak to soften; if we remember, we soak them in cold water overnight. If we forget, we use the quick soak method given below. Chickpeas can take a long time to cook, so be patient, they are worth the effort.

We make a big pot of these on Monday and eat them all week. On Wednesday we will simmer a big piece of tuna, or a couple of Italian sausages in the beans for a little change of pace.

1 pound dried chickpeas, or
  3–4 cups canned chickpeas
Salt
½ cup extra-virgin olive oil
2 onions, sliced
1 clove garlic, minced
4 anchovy filets
Pinch of crushed red pepper flakes

3 tablespoons tomato paste
One 28-ounce can San Marzano
  plum tomatoes
Pepper
1 handful fresh parsley leaves,
  finely chopped
8 fat lemon wedges, optional

To cook dried chickpeas, put them in a large pot and cover with water by 4 inches. Cover and bring to a rolling boil over high heat. Turn off the heat and allow the beans to soak undisturbed for about 1 hour. Drain the chickpeas and add fresh water to cover by 2 inches. Bring to a gentle boil over high heat, then reduce the heat to medium-low and cook until the beans are tender. Depending on the freshness of the beans, it can take anywhere from 1–3 hours. Test them after an hour to see how they are progressing. Add salt, and let them cool in their liquid.

Heat the olive oil in a large pan over medium heat. Add the onions and garlic and cook until the onions are soft, about 10 minutes. Add the anchovies, red pepper flakes, and tomato paste. Cook, stirring until the anchovies melt into the oil. Add the tomatoes and cook for 30 minutes. Add chickpeas and stir until everything is well mixed. Season with salt and pepper. Remove from heat and add the chopped parsley. Serve with lemon wedges, if you like.

# ZUCCA

When we are in Italy we try to live the Italian life. After all, what could be better? Every morning after breakfast we begin to think about lunch and dinner. We make a list, then check out where the local market will be. We know that within a ten-kilometre radius of our rented hilltop farmhouse, it will be market day in some nearby town. Pulling into town, it's never hard to find the market, they usually set up right in the town square. There under the pretty trees, vendors sell sunglasses, kitchenwares, aprons, and plastic shoes. And even though it happens every week, there is an air of festivity as the market rolls in and sets up with its porchetta truck, cheese wagon, fishmonger, and poultryman. Then, of course, there are the vegetables. It's funny in Italy, when you go to restaurants it seems there is hardly a vegetable in sight. But, of course, Italians eat vegetables at home and it's at markets like these, even in the cities, that they buy them. One day, while perusing the produce, we spotted a huge half pumpkin. We could see its deep orange flesh and judge its freshness by the way the seeds clung to its meaty walls. We quickly knew we wanted pumpkin but what would we do with so much? Just at that decisive moment, a little lady wearing an apron over her dress and a wool plaid coat the color of fall leaves, instructed the vendor to cut off a slice, which he happily did. Now it was our turn. We bought purple artichokes, long red peppers, and escarole, then pointed at the pumpkin. The vegetable man, dressed in a cerulean blue smock that matched his eyes, whipped out a knife like a Sumerian sickle sword and sliced us off a big thick wedge, just what we wanted. We cooked the pumpkin simply, as Ada Boni, the revered Italian cookbook author, advises. After all, this is home cooking.

We cut off the pumpkin peel, remove seeds and strings, and cut the flesh into 1-inch cubes. We store the pumpkin cubes in a plastic bag in the fridge, so they are ready to go when we want to cook them.

Heat ¼ cup extra-virgin olive oil in a heavy skillet over medium heat. Add 3 cloves crushed garlic and sauté until golden, then remove them from the skillet. Add 2 or 3 cups of pumpkin, some minced fresh rosemary or sage, a good pinch of salt, and a few grinds of pepper, and cook, stirring every now and then, until the pumpkin is tender, about 20 minutes. Sometimes we serve it with a squeeze of lemon. But sometimes we finish it with a splash of vinegar, a spoonful of sugar, and a handful of chopped fresh parsley and mint.

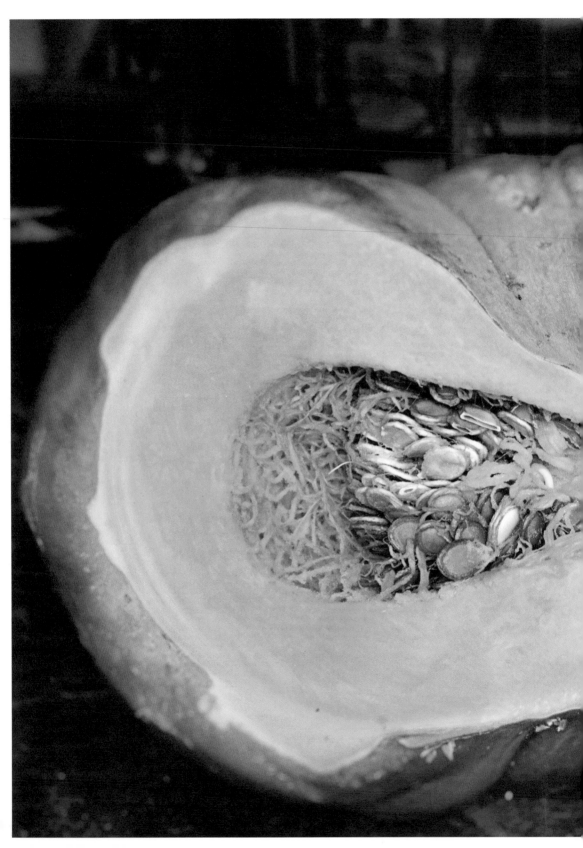

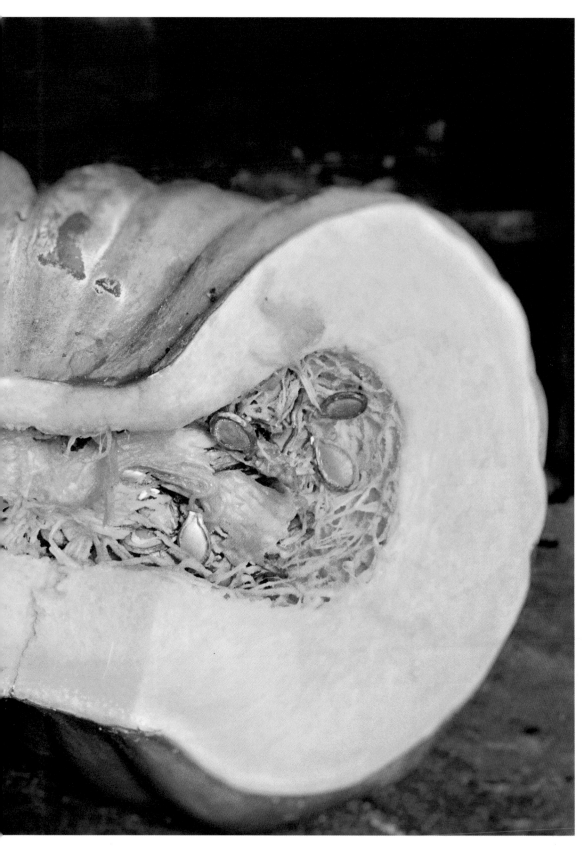

*Italian plum tomatoes used to make our Simple Tomato Sauce*

## WARM SALAD OF RADICCHIO & WHITE BEANS

In our pantry, we have a little bottle of 12-year-old *aceto balsamico tradizionale*, the expensive syrupy vinegar from Modena. We use it by the dropful in the traditional way—on steamed asparagus, fried eggs, and sweet strawberries. We break it out sometimes for this warm salad, where it tames the bitterness of the wilted radicchio. Younger, more affordable balsamic vinegars of very good quality and flavor are fine to use as well.

Put ½ cup really good extra-virgin olive oil, 1–2 cloves thinly sliced garlic, and 4 chopped anchovy filets into a medium nonreactive skillet or wide pot and warm over medium heat until fragrant, about 1 minute. Add the leaves from 2 heads quartered, rinsed radicchio and cook briefly, turning them as they begin to wilt. Add 2 cups cooked white beans with a spoonful of their cooking liquid or some water, season with salt and pepper, and cook, stirring gently now and again without breaking up the beans, just until the beans are warm and the radicchio is wilted, 3–5 minutes. Season with salt and pepper. Serve warm or at room temperature with a drizzle of more good olive oil and add a few drops of aged balsamic vinegar to each serving. ——*serves 6*

## CELERY BAKED WITH TOMATOES

Blanching celery brings out its sweet side. We serve this *contorno* as is or with crunchy golden bread crumbs sprinkled on top.

Preheat the oven to 375°. Separate the ribs from 1 head of celery, peel them with a vegetable peeler, and cut the ribs in half crosswise. Bring a medium pot of water to a boil and season generously with salt. Add the celery and simmer over medium-high heat until tender, 15–20 minutes. Drain them and transfer to a baking dish. Spoon 2 cups Simple Tomato Sauce (page 103) over the celery, drizzle with 2–3 tablespoons extra-virgin olive oil, and season with salt and pepper. Bake the celery until the tomato sauce thickens a bit and the celery is more tender, about 30 minutes. Drizzle with a little more olive oil. Serve warm or at room temperature. ——*serves 6*

why buy it when you can make it?

## SALSA VERDE

The Genovese classic, pesto, is perhaps the greatest of all the green sauces. But fresh basil is harder to find as the weather turns cold. So we make a sauce that's a cross between pesto and salsa verde. We don't mess around with machines much. We usually just mince, mash, and push sauces through sieves rather than pull out the Cuisinart, it's just how we are. But please feel free to process away! Try using a spice or electric coffee grinder to finely grind up the almonds, but in 2 batches so they don't turn into almond butter.

Put 3 anchovy filets, 2 tablespoons drained capers, 2 garlic cloves, ¼ teaspoon crushed red pepper flakes, the leaves of 1 bunch parsley, and 2 cups arugula in the bowl of a food processer. Process until finely chopped, then add ¼ cup ground roasted almonds, and process while you slowly add ½ cup really good extra-virgin olive oil. Transfer to a bowl and float a few tablespoons of olive oil on top to keep the salsa from turning dark. ——*makes 1½ cups*

## FRESH WHOLE MILK RICOTTA

We make ricotta all the time. It couldn't be easier. Ricotta means "twice cooked" in Italian because traditionally it's made from the whey left over when making mozzarella. We have used raw milk, goats' milk, organic milk, and supermarket milk, and it works out just fine.

Make a double boiler out of 2 large pots, with enough water in the bottom pot to come at least halfway up the sides of the top pot. Pour 1 gallon whole milk into the top pot and heat over medium-high heat until the temperature reaches 190° on a candy thermometer, about 15 minutes. Add 1 tablespoon salt, 1 cup plain yogurt, and ⅓ cup fresh lemon juice, and stir with a wooden spoon for about 30 seconds to mix everything together. Reduce the heat to low or turn it off. For the next 25 minutes, maintain the milk's temperature by lifting the pot out of the water if the milk gets too hot, or by returning it as the temperature drops. Don't stir the milk as the ricotta curds are forming. After about 25 minutes, use a skimmer to carefully lift all the ricotta curds out of the whey and transfer them to a fine-mesh strainer (no need to use cheesecloth) set over a bowl. Allow the ricotta to drain for about 1 hour, then pour off any of the drained whey from the bowl and gently dump the ricotta from the sieve into the bowl. Transfer to a covered container and use within 4 days. ——*makes 3 cups*

*Previous pages: left, Salsa Verde; right, Simple Tomato Sauce*

## SIMPLE TOMATO SAUCE
makes about 8 cups

We use the thicker version of this sauce for our Green Lasagne with Tomato Sauce & Fresh Ricotta (page 41), and the thinner version for saucing delicate fresh pasta, ravioli, and gnocchi. Or ladle it into soup bowls, float a fried egg on top, and sop up the goodness with warm crusty bread.

6 cups *passata di pomodoro,* strained tomatoes, or tomato purée

1 medium onion, halved

2–3 cloves garlic

4–6 tablespoons really good extra-virgin olive oil

Salt and pepper

Put the tomatoes into a heavy medium pot, rinsing out the containers with 4 cups of water and adding it to the pot. Add the onion halves, garlic, olive oil, and salt and pepper to taste to the pot. Gently simmer over medium-low heat for about 1 hour for a thin, loose sauce, or 2–3 hours for a richer, thicker consistency. Adjust the seasonings and add a little more olive oil to round out the flavors, if you like. Discard the onions and garlic before using.

# BALSAMELLA
## makes about 4 cups

One of the first sauces I learned to make when I began living on my own was béchamel, the classic French white sauce. Through practice, I learned to keep the butter from browning and the roux from taking on any color whatsoever. I loved its smooth, creamy whiteness, and how it tasted both nourishing and elegant. It went into all sorts of French dishes I was focused on then—savory gratins, the cheese soufflés I'd try out on my friends, the baked crêpes stuffed with chicken and seafood fillings. I'd add cheese to it and dress up simple things like poached eggs, steamed spinach and asparagus, and braised endives or fennel. Eventually, my interests expanded toward making Italian classics like lasagne and cannelloni, and there it was, my old friend with a new name, balsamella, as essential to these exquisite Italian dishes as it was to those French ones I'd learned to make years ago. ——MH

8 tablespoons butter
½ cup flour
4 cups hot milk

½ cup grated parmigiano-reggiano, optional
¼–½ teaspoon nutmeg
Salt

Melt the butter in a heavy medium saucepan over medium-low heat. Add the flour and cook for 1½–2 minutes, stirring constantly with a wooden spoon to prevent it from taking on any color. Gradually add the hot milk in a slow, steady stream, stirring constantly with a whisk to prevent lumps.

Increase the heat to medium and cook the sauce for 10–15 minutes, stirring constantly with a wooden spoon until it has the consistency of thick cream. Remove the pan from the heat. Stir in the cheese, if using, and season with nutmeg and salt to taste. Strain the sauce if it's lumpy. Lay a sheet of plastic wrap directly on the surface of the balsamella to keep it warm until ready to use and to prevent a skin from forming.

*Previous pages: left, Balsamella; right, Ragù Bolognese*

# RAGÙ BOLOGNESE
## makes about 6 cups

Like many long-simmered sauces, this one, perhaps the most delicious of all the Italian meat sauces, is more flavorful and balanced the following day.

2 tablespoons butter
2 tablespoons extra-virgin olive oil
1 onion, finely chopped
1 rib celery, finely diced
1 carrot, peeled and finely diced
2–3 thin slices prosciutto di Parma, finely chopped
2 chicken livers, finely chopped

¾ pound ground chuck
¾ pound ground pork
¼–½ whole nutmeg, finely grated
Salt and pepper
½ cup dry white wine
1 cup hot milk
One 28-ounce can tomato purée
1 cup chicken, veal, or beef stock

Heat the butter and oil in a heavy large pot over medium heat. Add the onions and cook, stirring frequently with a wooden spoon, just until soft and translucent, 3–5 minutes. Add the celery and carrots and cook until they begin to soften, about 3 minutes. Add the prosciutto and chicken livers and cook until the livers are pale pink, about 1 minute. Add the ground chuck and pork, season with nutmeg and salt and pepper, and cook, breaking up the meat with the back of the spoon, until there is still a little pink, about 5 minutes. Avoid frying or browning the meat.

Add the wine to the pot and cook until evaporated, 10–12 minutes. Add the milk, and cook over medium-low heat, stirring occasionally, until absorbed, about 20 minutes.

Meanwhile, heat the tomato purée and stock in a saucepan until hot, then add it to the meat. Reduce the heat to low and gently simmer, stirring occasionally, until the meat is tender, 6–7 hours. Add water, if needed, to keep the ragù loose and saucy. Season it with salt and pepper.

SPINACH TAGLIATELLE BOLOGNESE: Heat 4–6 cups Ragù Bolognese in a wide pan over medium heat until hot. Add 1 pound cooked fresh spinach tagliatelle and a little of the pasta water. Serve with grated parmigiano. —— *serves 4–8*

PAPPARDELLE BOLOGNESE: Substitute fresh pappardelle for spinach tagliatelle.

dolci

# APPLE CAKE
serves 8–10

We first ate this cake in the fruitful Val di Non in Trentino, where orchards abound. Back home we didn't know which apple variety to use, so we called Karen Bates, of the Philo Apple Farm in the Anderson Valley in California, who passed on these tips: Early apples tend to break down very easily—great for applesauce and very tender, juicy pies. Mid-season apples cook up fairly tender and hold their shape, while late-season apples border on staying a little too firm and are a lot less juicy. So make your applesauce early in the season and store your late apples as long as you can. We decided on Golden Delicious for their rich perfume and the ability to hold their shape when cooked.

6 tablespoons butter, at room temperature, plus more for the pan

1½ cups flour, plus more for the pan

¾ cup granulated sugar, plus more for the apples

1 egg

1 teaspoon vanilla extract

2 teaspoons baking powder

1 pinch of salt

½ cup milk

Grated zest of 2 lemons

2–3 Golden Delicious apples, peeled, cored, and thickly sliced

Powdered sugar

Preheat oven to 350°. Butter and flour a 9-inch springform pan. Beat the butter in a large mixing bowl with an electric mixer until creamy. Gradually add the sugar and beat until fluffy, then beat in the egg. Add the vanilla.

Whisk together the flour, baking powder, and salt in a bowl. Add the flour to the butter mixture gradually, alternating with the milk in thirds, beating well after each addition. Stir in the zest. Pour the batter into the prepared pan, and smooth the surface with a spatula.

Starting from the outside, arrange the apple slices in a circle standing them on end with the narrow point in the batter, then fill in the center with as many slices as you can fit. The apples should be quite close together and cover most of the batter. Sprinkle 2 tablespoons granulated sugar over the apples.

Bake for 50–60 minutes, until a toothpick inserted into the cake (not the apples) comes out clean. Place on a rack, remove the outer ring, and allow the cake to cool. Dust the cake with powdered sugar just before serving, if you like.

# JAM TART
makes one 9-inch tart

Use a concentrated jam that's full of flavor for this simple tart. No need to weave the strips for the lattice top. Do as the Italians do, just twist them—*bellissima!*

FOR THE PASTRY
2 cups flour
¼ cup superfine sugar
1 teaspoon salt
8 tablespoons unsalted butter, diced
1 egg

1 egg yolk
1 tablespoon white wine

FOR THE TART
¾–1 cup fruit jam, such as apricot, plum, or sour cherry
1 egg, lightly beaten with a little water

For the pastry, mix together the flour, sugar, and salt in a large bowl. Add the butter and work it in with a pastry blender or the tips of your fingers until the mixture resembles wet sand. Lightly beat the egg and yolk together. Add the eggs and wine to the dough until it just holds together. Don't overwork or dough will be tough. Wrap dough in plastic and refrigerate for at least 1 hour.

We prefer to make dough by hand, but you can use a food processor: put the flour, sugar, and salt in the work bowl, process for a few seconds to mix, then add the butter and pulse a few times until the mixture resembles wet sand. Add the egg, egg yolk, and wine and process a few seconds more to form the dough. Don't overprocess. Wrap in plastic and refrigerate as described above.

Preheat the oven to 375°. Roll out two-thirds of the dough on a lightly floured surface to an ⅛-inch thickness. Wrap the dough around the rolling pin, then lay it in a 9-inch tart pan with a removable bottom. Cut off the excess. Prick the pastry bottom all over with a fork. Spread the jam over the bottom of the tart.

Roll out the remaining pastry on a lightly floured surface. Use a sharp knife to cut ¼-inch-wide strips. Lightly twist and lay the strips in a diagonal lattice on top of the jam. Trim the strips to just inside the tart shell, then gently press the outside edge of the crust down over the ends of the strips. Brush the pastry with the egg wash.

Bake the tart until golden, about 25 minutes. Remove the warm tart from the pan and allow it to cool on a rack.

# CHEESECAKE FROM ROME'S JEWISH QUARTER
## serves 8

This tender cake, sometimes referred to as a pudding *(budino di ricotta)* started out as a pancake. Food historian Clifford Wright notes that Sicilian Jews took their traditions of making and cooking with ricotta to Rome when they were expelled from Sicily in the fifteenth century and a version of this recipe came with them. You can still find this delicious dessert in Rome's Jewish quarter in its simplest form—eggs, sugar, ricotta and cinnamon. In our recipe, we separate the eggs and fold in the beaten whites, which makes the cake even more delicate. If you can't find good quality fresh ricotta, make your own (page 102).

1 tablespoon butter
¼ cup fine fresh bread crumbs
5 eggs, separated
¾ cup sugar
3 tablespoons cake flour
1 teaspoon salt

½ teaspoon cinnamon
2 cups fresh whole milk ricotta
 (page 102)
¼ cup Grand Marnier
Grated zest of 1 lemon

Preheat the oven to 350°. Grease the bottom and sides of a 9-inch springform pan with the butter, then dust the pan with the bread crumbs.

Beat the egg yolks with the sugar, flour, salt, and cinnamon in a large mixing bowl with an electric mixer until creamy, about 5 minutes. Process the ricotta, Grand Marnier, and zest in a food processor until smooth. Fold the ricotta into the egg mixture, using a rubber spatula, until the batter is well mixed.

In another mixing bowl, beat the egg whites with a whisk, or an electric mixer fitted with a whisk, until frothy. Add a little squeeze of lemon juice and continue to beat until the whites are stiff but not dry. Fold one-third of the whites into the batter, then gently fold in the remaining whites, in two batches, taking care not to overmix, which will cause the whites to deflate.

Pour the ricotta batter into the prepared pan. Bake until golden and firm to the touch, about 40 minutes. Remove the cake from the oven and transfer to a rack. It will sink as it cools. This cake is best served warm or at room temperature. It loses a little flavor when it is refrigerated.

# VIN SANTO–POACHED PEARS WITH GORGONZOLA DOLCE
serves 4–8

For poaching these pears, we like to use any number of Italian *passiti*, or sweet dessert wines—vin santo from Tuscany, Recioto di Soave from the Veneto, and many of the Italian (nonsparkling) *moscati*. The delicate flavors and the prices vary: choose one that suits your taste and budget. But the beautifully creamy, greenish blue-veined cheese should come from its namesake town in Lombardy.

4 semifirm, ripe pears

1 lemon, juiced and its zest cut into wide strips

1½ cups sweet Italian dessert wine, such as vin santo, Dindarello, or Moscato

1 vanilla bean, split lengthwise

8–12 ounces Gorgonzola Dolce, at room temperature

Peel the pears, leaving the stems intact. Rub them with lemon juice to prevent them from turning brown and cut them in half lengthwise. Use a melon baller or a small teaspoon to scoop out the core and seeds.

Arrange the pears cut side down in a heavy wide pot just large enough so they fit in one layer. Add the wine and enough water (about 3 cups) to barely cover the fruit. Add the vanilla bean and lemon zest. Lay a piece of parchment paper directly on top of the pears and cover the pot with the lid. Bring the liquid to a simmer over medium heat. Reduce the heat to low and poach the pears until they feel meaty and tender when pierced, 15–30 minutes, depending on variety and ripeness.

Transfer the pears to a serving platter, cut side up, and cover them with the parchment paper. Remove and discard the vanilla bean and zest from the poaching liquid. Boil the liquid over medium-high heat until it has reduced to a nice syrupy consistency, 20–30 minutes. Remove the parchment paper and pour the syrup over the pears. Let the pears sit at room temperature for an hour or so before serving so they can absorb some of the syrupy juices.

Serve each pear with a wedge of the Gorgonzola in a wide dessert dish, spooning some of the fragrant juices over them.

# CHOCOLATE CHESTNUT TORTE
makes one 10-inch cake

We serve this earthy, delicate chocolate cake with tea in the afternoon or for dessert during the holidays with chilled flutes of Moscato d'Asti.

2 cups whole milk

2½ cups peeled whole chestnuts, vacuum-packed or in a jar

1 cup blanched almonds, toasted and finely ground

5 ounces bittersweet chocolate, coarsely chopped

9 tablespoons unsalted butter, at room temperature

½ cup sugar

5 eggs, separated

Powdered sugar

Bring the milk almost to a boil in a medium pot over medium heat. Add the chestnuts and remove the pot from the heat. Cover and let them steep to soften for 30 minutes. Drain the chestnuts, discarding the milk. Chop the chestnuts neither too fine, nor too coarse. Transfer to a medium bowl and add the almonds and chocolate, and gently stir to combine. Set aside.

Preheat the oven to 350°. Grease a 10-inch springform pan with a little butter. Line the bottom of the pan with parchment paper, then grease the paper, using a little more butter. Set the pan aside.

Beat the remaining 8 tablespoons of the butter and ¼ cup of the sugar together in a large mixing bowl with an electric mixer on medium-high speed until light and fluffy. Add the egg yolks one at a time, beating well after each addition. Add the chestnut mixture and stir until well combined. Set aside.

Beat the egg whites in another large mixing bowl with an electric mixer on high speed until frothy. Gradually add the remaining ¼ cup of sugar, beating until stiff, shiny peaks form. Fold the whites into the batter in thirds. Pour the batter into the prepared pan. Bake until the cake is set and a toothpick inserted into the center comes out clean, 50–60 minutes.

Let the cake cool on a rack before removing it from the pan. To remove it, invert the cake onto a small baking sheet. Remove the pan bottom and parchment paper, then invert the cake onto a cake plate. Dust the cake with powdered sugar just before serving. It's extra-lovely with dollops of unsweetened whipped cream.

# MONTE BIANCO
serves 8

During the holidays we always serve a classic dessert that presents with a certain celebratory drama. This delicate mountain of sieved chestnuts with bits of chocolate, capped with drifts of whipped cream, is one of them. It's a playful homage to Mont Blanc, the highest peak in the Alps (and Europe), with one foot in Valle d'Aosta, Italy's smallest region, and one foot in France.

3 cups milk
1 vanilla bean, split lengthwise
4–5 cups peeled whole chestnuts, vacuum-packed or in a jar, quartered
2 tablespoons unsweetened cocoa
½ cup kirschwasser or rum

4 ounces bittersweet chocolate, chopped
2 cups heavy cream
3 tablespoons granulated sugar
1 teaspoon vanilla extract
Powdered sugar

Bring the milk and vanilla bean almost to a boil in a medium pot over medium heat. Remove from the heat and add the chestnuts. Cover and let the chestnuts steep to soften for 30 minutes. Drain the chestnuts, discarding the milk and vanilla pod. Return them to the pot and stir in the cocoa and liquor.

Working over a large wide sheet of waxed paper, pass the chestnuts through a potato ricer or food mill, showering them onto the paper. Pass them through a second time to make them lighter and more delicate. Lift up the corners of the paper and gently sprinkle about a quarter of the chestnuts onto a cake stand or serving platter in a mound. Sprinkle one-third of the chocolate over the mound. Repeat the layering process three more times, ending with a layer of chestnuts. Each layer will make the mound taller. Very gently shape the mound, careful not to pack down its delicate texture, into a pointed peak.

Whip the cream, granulated sugar, and vanilla together in a bowl to soft peaks. Cover the top two-thirds of the peak with half of the whipped cream, making swirls to resemble snowdrifts. The dessert can be refrigerated, uncovered, for up to 2 hours before serving. Dust it with powdered sugar just before serving. Slice or spoon wedges of the mountain with the snow onto dessert plates, adding a dollop of the remaining whipped cream to each serving.

## GELATO DI GIANDUIA
makes about 1 quart

In any form, the classic Piedmontese combination of toasted hazelnuts and chocolate is one of our favorite flavors. You'll see why, when you taste this luxurious gelato.

3 cups skinned hazelnuts
2¼ cups whole milk
1¼ cups heavy cream
¾ cup sugar
6 egg yolks

Pinch of salt
6 tablespoons unsweetened cocoa
1 tablespoon Frangelico or other
   hazelnut liqueur
2 teaspoons vanilla extract

Heat the oven to 350° and toast the hazelnuts on a baking sheet until deep golden brown, about 15 minutes. When cool, finely grind 2 cups of the nuts in a food processor. Chop the remaining 1 cup of nuts and set them aside.

Put the milk and cream into a saucepan and bring to a simmer over medium heat. Remove the pan from the heat, stir in the finely ground hazelnuts, and steep for 1 hour. Strain through a fine-mesh sieve into another saucepan, pressing on the solids before discarding them. Add ½ cup of the sugar to the milk. Bring to a simmer over medium heat, stirring until the sugar dissolves.

Put the yolks, salt, and the remaining ¼ cup of sugar into a medium mixing bowl and whisk together until thick and pale yellow. Whisk in the cocoa. Gradually ladle about 1 cup of the hot milk into the yolks, whisking constantly. Stir the warm yolk mixture into the hot milk in the saucepan. Reduce the heat to low, and cook, stirring constantly, until the custard is thick enough to coat the back of the spoon and registers between 175° and 180° on an instant-read thermometer, 3–5 minutes.

Strain the custard into a medium bowl. Add the liqueur and vanilla and stir frequently until cooled. Cover and refrigerate until completely chilled, about 4 hours. This will keep in the refrigerator for up to 2 days.

Churn the custard in an ice-cream maker following the manufacturer's directions. Just before the gelato has finished churning, add the reserved chopped hazelnuts, letting the paddle stir them in. Transfer the gelato to a quart container with a lid. Cover and freeze for a couple of hours or until it is just firm.

OUR WEBSITE

Our website, thecanalhouse.com, a companion to this book, offers our readers ways to get the best from grocery stores and markets (what and how to buy, how to store it, cook it, and serve it). We'll tell you why a certain cut of meat works for a particular recipe; which boxes, cans, bottles, or tins are worthwhile; which apples are best for baking; and what to look for when buying olive oil, salt, or butter. We'll also suggest what's worth seeking out from specialty stores or mail-order sources and why. And wait, there's more. We share our stories, the wines we are drinking, gardening tips, and events; and our favorite books, cooks, and restaurants are on our site—take a look.